S0-AYA-971

World Link

Developing English Fluency

Video Course

Susan Stempleski

Educational Linguistics
Library

THOMSON
™

Australia · Canada · Mexico · Singapore · Spain · United Kingdom · United States

World Link Video Workbook Intro
Susan Stempleski

Publisher: *Christopher Wenger*
Director of Product Marketing: *Amy Mabley*
Director of Product Development: *Anita Raducanu*
International Marketing Manager: *Ian Martin*
Acquisitions Editor: *Mary Sutton-Paul*
Development Editor: *Rebecca Klevberg*
Associate Editor: *Christine Galvin-Combet*
Editorial Assistant: *Bridget McLaughlin*
Production Manager: *Sally Giangrande*

Sr. Print Buyer: *Mary Beth Hennebury*
Compositor: *Pre-Press Company, Inc.*
Project Manager: *MaryBeth Cameron*
Copyeditor: *Margaret Hines*
Photo Researcher: *Nick Raducanu*
Cover/Text Designer: *Christopher Hanzie, TYA, Inc.*
Cover Image: *TYA Inc. PhotoDisc, Inc.*
Printer: *China Translation & Printing Services Ltd.*

Printed in China
3 4 5 6 7 8 9 10 — 09 08 07

For more information contact Thomson ELT,
25 Thomson Place, Boston, MA 02210 USA, or you
can visit our Internet site at elt.thomson.com

ISBN-13: 978-0-7593-9638-8
ISBN-10: 0-7593-9638-8

Acknowledgements

We would like to thank the educators who provided invaluable feedback during the development of the World Link Video Course:
Judy Hardacre de Cerqueira, Instituto Cultural Brasil Estados Unidos; Raquel Cristina dos Santos Faria, Empresas MAI de Ensino Ltda; Yeh Chin, Takming College; Jeongwan Lim, Myongji University; Litany Pires Ribeiro, Cultura Inglesa Belo Horizonte; Maria Teresa Mineiro de Mello Vianna, Greenwich Schools; Cynthia Yu, Soochow University

Photo Credits

Unless noted below, all photos are from the World Link Video Program.
3: TL, TR, BM, BR: Hemera Photo Objects; TM: © Richard T. Nowitz/CORBIS; BL: © Royalty-Free/CORBIS 6: TL: © Royalty-Free/Index Stock Imagery, Inc.; TR: © Yang Liu/CORBIS; BL,BM: ©Royalty-Free/Index Stock Imagery, Inc.; BR © Royalty-Free/CORBIS 7: M: © Larry Lawfer/Index Stock Imagery, Inc. 8: TL: Royalty-Free/Index Stock Imagery, Inc.; TM: © Image Source Limited/Index Stock Imagery, Inc.; TR: © Photos.com/Index Stock Imagery, Inc. 9: L: © Frank Trapper/CORBIS; M: © Frank Trapper/CORBIS; R © Stephane Cardinale/CORBIS 11: All: Hemera Photo Objects 14: TL: © Patrick Giardino/CORBIS; TR: © PhotoLibrary.com pty. Ltd./ Index Stock Imagery, Inc.; BL: © DesignPics, Inc./Index Stock Imagery, Inc.; BR © Lonnie Duka/ Index Stock Imagery, Inc. 15: ML and MR: Hemera Photo Objects 19: TL: © Nicholas Eveleigh/SuperStock; TML: © Reuters/CORBIS; TMR, TR: Hemera Photo Objects; BL: © HIRB/Index Stock Imagery, Inc.; BML, BMR, BR: Hemera Photo Objects 22: TL: Hemera Photo Objects; TR: © Jose Luis Pelaez, Inc./CORBIS; BL: © Gary D. Landsman/CORBIS; BM: © Peter M. Fisher/CORBIS; BR: © PictureNet/CORBIS 24: T: All Hemera Photo Objects 25: L and M: Hemera Photo Objects; R: © Toru Hani/Reuters/CORBIS 27: TL: © DesignPics, Inc./Index Stock Imagery, Inc.; TML: © Shannon Stapleton/Reuters/CORBIS; TMR and TR: Hemera Photo Objects; B: All Hemera Photo Objects 30: All: Hemera Photo Objects 32: L: Hemera Photo Objects; R: © HIRB/ Index Stock Imagery, Inc. 35: M and B: Hemera Photo Objects 38: TL: © Vstock LLC/Index Stock Imagery, Inc.; TR: Royalty-Free/Index Stock Imagery, Inc.; BL: © Gary Conner/Index Stock Imagery, Inc.; BM: © Pixland/Index Stock Imagery, Inc.; BR Royalty-Free/Index Stock Imagery, Inc.; 40: All: Hemera Photo Objects 43: L: Mitch Diamond/Index Stock Imagery, Inc.; M: ThinkStock LLC/Index Stock Imagery, Inc.; R © James Lafayette/Index Stock Imagery, Inc. 46: TL: © Omni Photo Communications, Inc./Index Stock Imagery, Inc.; TR and BL: Hemera Photo Objects; BR: © PhotoLibrary.com pty. Ltd./Index Stock Imagery, Inc. 48: MedioImages, Inc./Index Stock Imagery, Inc.; 51: TL: Hemera Photo Objects; TML: Matthew Borkoski/Index Stock Imagery, Inc.; TMR: ThinkStock LLC/Index Stock Imagery, Inc.; TR: DesignPics, Inc./Index Stock Imagery, Inc.; ML: Royalty-Free/Index Stock Imagery, Inc.; MML: Barry Winiker/Index Stock Imagery, Inc.; MMR: © HIRB/Index Stock Imagery, Inc.; MR: © Ted Wilcox/Index Stock Imagery, Inc.; B: Royalty-Free/Index Stock Imagery, Inc. 54: T and B: Hemera Photo Objects 56: TL: © Tom Stewart/CORBIS; TML: Royalty-Free/Index Stock Imagery, Inc.; TMR: © T. Reed/Plus Studios/CORBIS; TR: © Darama/CORBIS; ML: © Royalty-Free/CORBIS; MML: © Royalty-Free/CORBIS; MMR © Cameron/CORBIS; MR © Steve Prezant/CORBIS 59: © Philip Gould/CORBIS 62: T: Hemera Photo Objects; B: © Medio Images, Inc./Index Stock Imagery, Inc. 64: L: Gary Conner/Index Stock Imagery, Inc.; M: DesignPics, Inc./Index Stock Imagery, Inc.; R Barry Winniker/Index Stock Imagery, Inc. 67: TL: PhotoAlto/SuperStock; TR: © Diaphor Agency/Index Stock Imagery, Inc.; BL: © Medio-Images/SuperStock; BM: © DesignPics, Inc.; BR Royalty-Free/CORBIS 70: L: Lonnie Duka/Index Stock Imagery, Inc.; M, R: Royalty-Free/Index Stock Imagery, Inc. 72: TL: HIRB/Index Stock Imagery, Inc.; TML and TMR: Hemera Photo Objects; TR: AbleStock/Index Stock Imagery, Inc.; 75: All: Hemera Photo Objects 78: T: PhotoLibrary.com pty. Ltd./Index Stock Imagery, Inc.; B: © Michael Keller/CORBIS 81: TL, TML, TM, TMR: Hemera Photo Objects; TR: © Lee Snider/Photo Images/CORBIS 83: All: Hemera Photo Objects 86: T: © Image Source Limited/Index Stock Imagery, Inc.; B: © Peter Langone/Index Stock Imagery, Inc. 88: TL, TML, TM, TR,: Hemera Photo Objects; TMR: © Royalty-Free/CORBIS 91: TL: © Tomas del Almo/Index Stock Imagery, Inc.; TML: © David Pollack/CORBIS; TM: © DesignPics, Inc./Index Stock Imagery, Inc.; TMR: Hemera Photo Objects; TR: A. Huber/U. Starke/Index Stock Imagery, Inc.; BL: © Patricia Barry Levy/Index Stock Imagery, Inc.; BML: Hemera Photo Objects: BM Royalty-Free/CORBIS; BMR HIRB/Index Stock Imagery, Inc.; BR © Image Source Limited/Index Stock Imagery, Inc. 94: © Image Source Limited/Index Stock Imagery, Inc.

Welcome to the *World Link* Video Course! This new video series creates interesting and fun opportunities for learners to become fluent in everyday English. The video program is part of the *World Link* textbook series, a four-level core series for young adult and adult learners of English from the beginning to intermediate level. The video course consists of four sixty-minute videos, which can be used in conjunction with the *World Link* textbooks, or as the basis of a stand-alone course in the language lab or classroom when used with the *World Link* Video Workbook.

The *World Link* Videos

Each of the World Link Videos contains twelve video units. Each video unit consists of an original dramatic episode with real-life interviews and is divided into two segments, **City Living** and **Global Viewpoints**.

- **City Living** segments are short, entertaining episodes about six friends from different countries living, studying, and working in exciting New York City.

- **Global Viewpoints** segments feature real-life interviews with students and professionals from around the world. These interviews offer examples of real English language use while presenting viewpoints from a wide variety of cultural backgrounds.

The *World Link* Video Workbooks

Each video workbook has twelve eight-page units, each unit divided into two main parts that correspond to the video units. The first part focuses on the **City Living** episode, while the second focuses on the **Global Viewpoints** interviews.

City Living

The six-page **City Living** part of the unit is made up of four sections:

- **Preview** - This one-page section uses still photos from the video, speech bubbles, and a short comprehension activity to preview key moments in the episode.

- **Before You Watch** - This one-page section presents and previews key vocabulary used in the episode.

- **While You Watch** - This two-page section includes viewing activities designed to increase understanding of the language and storyline of the episode.

- **After You Watch** - This two-page section includes follow-up language exercises focusing on grammar and useful expressions from the video.

Global Viewpoints

The two-page **Global Viewpoints** part of the unit is made up of one or two groups of interviews. For each group of interviews there is a **Before You Watch** section focusing on needed vocabulary, and a **While You Watch** section focusing on video comprehension. The final section, **Your View,** asks for personal responses to questions about issues related to the theme of the entire unit.

Real English boxes appear throughout each unit and explain cultural points or colloquial language points that appear in the **City Living** and **Global Viewpoints**

I have really enjoyed working on the *World Link* Video Course, and I hope learners have as much fun using it. My greatest hope is that the World Link Video Course helps many, many learners become confident and fluent speakers of English.

Sincerely,
Susan Stempleski

The *World Link* Video Characters

"City Living" is the story of the day-to-day lives of six friends living, studying, and working in New York City. Takeshi Mifune is a film student from Osaka, Japan. He lives with his best friend Mike Johnson, a struggling actor from Minneapolis, Minnesota. Tara Greene is a student and waitress from Nottingham, England. Her roommates are Sun-hee Park, a computer instructor from Seoul, Korea, and Claudia Oliveira, a software sales manager from Rio de Janeiro, Brazil. Claudia's boyfriend, Roberto Chavez, is a financial analyst from Mexico City, Mexico. Interesting, exciting, and always fun—that's "City Living"!

Name: Takeshi Mifune
Age: 26
Hometown: Osaka, Japan
Profession: film student

Name: Sun-hee Park
Age: 25
Hometown: Seoul, Korea
Profession: computer
              instructor

Name: Mike Johnson
Age: 24
Hometown: Minneapolis,
              Minnesota, U.S.A.
Profession: actor, waiter, singer,
              painter, receptionist

Name: Claudia Oliveira
Age: 29
Hometown: Rio de Janeiro,
              Brazil
Profession: software sales
              manager

Name: Tara Greene
Age: 27
Hometown: Nottingham,
              England, U.K.
Profession: art student,
              waitress

Name: Roberto Chavez
Age: 28
Hometown: Mexico City,
              Mexico
Profession: financial
              analyst

World Link Video Workbook Intro

1 Greetings and Intros

City Living | Please, call me Dave.

1 Preview

 A In this episode, Mike, Tara, Takeshi, and Claudia talk about famous people.

Mike doesn't like his name.

Takeshi makes a video of Tara and Mike.

Tara joins the fun.

But Claudia isn't happy.

B Look at the photos above. Then complete the sentences with *a*, *b*, or *c*.

1. Mike thinks his name is _____.

   a. good   b. bad   c. famous

2. Takeshi has a _____.

   a. video camera   b. cell phone   c. computer

3. Tara is _____.

   a. a famous movie star   b. really Jennifer Lopez   c. having fun

4. Claudia is _____.

   a. happy   b. angry   c. fine

2 Before You Watch

A Here are some words you will hear in the video. Write the correct word or words under each picture.

> news reporter   sunglasses   actor/actress
> doorbell   phone number   singer

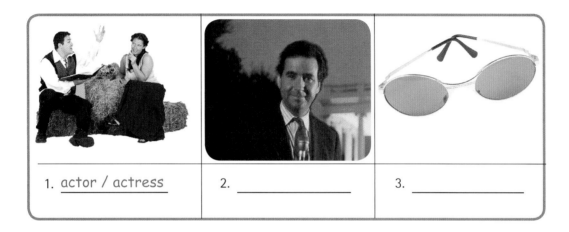

1. <u>actor / actress</u>

2. _____

3. _____

4. _____

5. _____

6. _____

B Here are some more words you will hear in the video. Unscramble the words in parentheses to complete the sentences.

1. Keanu Reeves is a cool ___movie star___. (imove rats)

2. Katie Couric is a _____ news reporter. (sumafo)

3. Jennifer Aniston is my _____ actress. (ravofiet)

4. David Beckham is a really good _____. (crocse replya)

5. Jennifer Lopez is a _____ singer. (terga)

A What happens? Watch the video. Number the pictures from 1 to 5 to put them in order.

OK, Mr. Movie Star.

Mike! Takeshi! Tara!

Hi! I'm Keanu Reeves.

We're late for the movie!

Actors have great names.

 B What do you hear? Watch the video again. Circle the words you hear.

1. Mike: Tom Cruise. Harrison Ford. Actors have (great) / famous names.

2. Mike: People / They call me Bond. James Bond.

3. Tara: . . . and my / your name's Jennifer Lopez!

4. Tara: . . . and here we have the famous / my favorite soccer player David Beckham.

5. Mike: But, please, call me / him Dave.

6. Claudia: And I'm / call me Julia Roberts.

What do they say? Watch the video. Write the words you hear to complete the conversations.

Excuse me? *My phone number?*

Real English

Tara says *Excuse me?* to show she is surprised at Mike's question.

Mike:	Tom Cruise. Harrison Ford. Actors have great names. (1) _I'm_ an
	actor, and (2)_____ name's Mike Johnson.
Tara:	What's a great (3)_____?
Mike:	(4)_____ don't know. But I want a great name.

· ·

Mike:	Hi, (5)_____ Keanu Reeves. Nice to meet you.
Tara:	. . . and my name's Jennifer Lopez! But you can (6)_____ me J-Lo.
Mike:	OK, J-Lo. Nice to meet you. (7)_____ my favorite actress and (8)_____.

· ·

Tara:	Hmm . . . are (9)_____ Jim Carrey?
Mike:	No. (10)_____ Jackie Chan.
Tara:	Oh (11)_____, you're (12)_____.

A Study the expressions from the video in the box below. Then use the expressions to complete the conversations. Use each expression only once.

Useful Expressions

Please call me . . .

What's your phone number?

(It's) nice to meet you, too.

My name's . . .

What's your name?

1. A: It's nice to meet you.
B: Nice to meet you, too.

2. A: _____
B: My name's Hiroko Tanaka.

3. A: I'm Michael Conner.
_____ Mike.
B: OK, Mike.

4. A: Hi. My name's Jay.
What's your name?
B: _____ Paul.

5. A: _____
B: It's 555-7794.

B Number the sentences from 1 to 5 to put the conversation in order.

_____ My name's Matthew, but please call me Matt.

_____ Nice to meet you, too.

_____ Yes, I am. My name's Gina. What's your name?

___1___ Hi! Are you in this class?

_____ OK, Matt. Nice to meet you.

Language Link: Contractions with *be* and possessive adjectives	
Contractions with *be*	Possessive adjectives
I am = I'm	my
you are = you're	your
she is = she's	her
he is = he's	his
it is = it's	its

I'm *an actor and* my *name's Mike Johnson.*

 C In the video, Mike uses a contraction and a possessive adjective to talk about himself. Study the box. Then complete the conversations.

1. Kim: Hi! (1)_____My_____ name is Kim. (2)_____ a student in this class.

What's (3)_____ name?

Mia: (4)_____ Mia. This is (5)_____ friend. (6)_____ name is

Susan. (7)_____ a student in this class, too.

2. Pete: Hey Tracy. Who's (8)_____ English

teacher this year?

Tracy: (9)_____ name is Tom Berry.

(10)_____ very nice.

D Complete the story summary. Use the words in the box.

~~actor~~   news reporter   doorbell   great   movie   soccer player   phone number   sunglasses

Mike is an (1)_____actor_____. His real name is Mike

Johnson, but he wants a (2)_____ name. Mike puts

on (3)_____ and acts like Keanu Reeves. Tara acts

like Jennifer Lopez and Mike asks for her (4)_____.

Later they act like a (5)_____ and (6)_____.

Claudia rings the (7)_____. She calls, "Mike! Takeshi!

Tara!" Claudia comes to the apartment and says, "Come on,

you three. We're late for the (8)_____."

Greetings and Intros

Global Viewpoints | Introductions

1 Before You Watch

 A Here are some words you will hear in the interviews about "Introductions." Use the words in the box to complete the sentences.

| computer engineer | first name | last name | ~~nickname~~ | spelled | student |

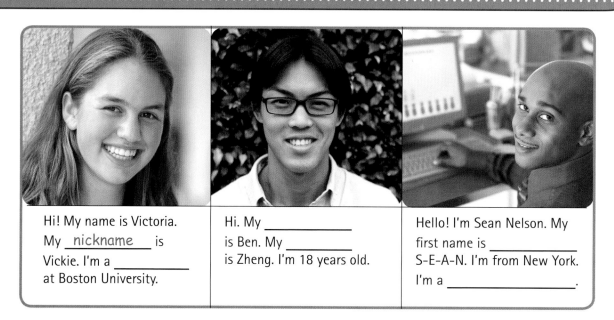

Hi! My name is Victoria. My _nickname_ is Vickie. I'm a _____ at Boston University.

Hi. My _____ is Ben. My _____ is Zheng. I'm 18 years old.

Hello! I'm Sean Nelson. My first name is _____ S-E-A-N. I'm from New York. I'm a _____ .

2 While You Watch

 Watch the interviews and circle *True* or *False*. Then correct the false sentences.

1. Woo Sung's last name is Chung.   True   False

2. Dayanne's nickname is spelled D-A-I.   True   False

3. Jonathan's nickname is Johnny.   True   False

4. Agnes's last name is spelled T-O-U-N-K-A-R-A.   True   False

5. Brad's last name is Fish.   True   False

6. Calum is a student at Boston University.   True   False

7. Jonathan is a computer engineer.   True   False

8. Hana is 19 years old.   True   False

Real English

...I am a student at Harvard University

Harvard University is the oldest university in the U.S. It opened in 1636 in Cambridge, Massachusetts.

Global Viewpoints | People We Like

1 Before You Watch

Here are three names you will hear in the interviews about "People We Like." Write the correct name under each picture.

(Angelina Jolie) (Antonio Banderas) (Julia Roberts)

1. _____ 2. _____ 3. _____

2 While You Watch

 Now watch the interviews. What do these people say? Circle the correct words.

1. Dayanne: My favorite <u>actor / actress</u> is <u>Angelina Jolie / Antonio Banderas</u>.

2. Woo Sung: My favorite <u>actor / actress</u> is <u>Antonio Banderas / Julia Roberts</u>.

3. Kevin: My favorite actress is <u>Julia Roberts / Angelina Jolie</u> because I think she is the most beautiful <u>woman / actress</u> in the world.

Your View on . . . *Greetings and Intros*
How about you? Fill in the blanks with your own information.

First name: _____

Last name: _____

Phone number: _____

Favorite actor/actress:_____

Favorite singer: _____

2 Countries and Nationalities

City Living | Where is it?

1 Preview

 A In this episode, the six friends play an interesting game.

Let's play "Where is it?"

Tara wants to play her favorite game.

... this game is so boring!

Claudia has a different opinion.

What city is it? It's in South America ...

Roberto takes a turn.

It's expensive ... and cheap.

Sun-hee gives a difficult hint.

B Look at the photos above. Then complete the sentences with *a*, *b*, or *c*.

1. Tara _____ playing "Where is it?"

    a. likes   b. doesn't like   c. hates

2. _____ thinks the game is boring.

    a. Tara   b. Sun-hee   c. Claudia

3. Roberto and Sun-hee give hints about _____.

    a. places   b. people   c. the game

4. Sun-hee's hint is not _____.

    a. interesting   b. easy   c. cheap

2 Before You Watch

 A Here are some words you will hear in the video. Write the words in the chart.

> Beijing   Brasilia   ~~Brazilian~~   China
> Japanese   Korean   Mexican   the U.S.

	Country	Nationality	Capital City
	Brazil	Brazilian	
		Chinese	
	Japan		Tokyo
	Korea		Seoul
	Mexico		Mexico City
		American	Washington, DC

B Here are some more words you will hear in the video. Match the words with their opposites.

1. beautiful _b_
2. big ___
3. boring ___
4. cheap ___
5. crowded ___
6. easy ___
7. modern ___
8. noisy ___

a. interesting
b. ~~ugly~~
c. empty
d. difficult
e. expensive
f. quiet
g. small
h. old

A What's the story? Watch the video and number the sentences from 1 to 6 to put them in order. Then write the sentences in the correct order below.

___ Roberto asks a question about Rio de Janeiro.

___ Claudia says the game is exciting.

___ Claudia answers Sun-hee's question.

_1_ The group starts to play "Where is it?"

___ Claudia says the game is boring.

___ Sun-hee asks a question about New York.

1. The group starts to play "Where is it?"

2. _____

3. _____

4. _____

5. _____

6. _____

 B Who is speaking? Watch the video again. Circle the answers.

1. OK. Game time! Let's play "Where is it?"   Claudia / Mike / (Tara)

2. Beijing is a famous city there.   Claudia / Mike / Tara

3. Are you from São Paulo?   Claudia / Mike / Tara

4. I know. It's right here. It's New York City!   Claudia / Mike / Tara

5. Wait a minute! "This game is so boring!"   Claudia / Mike / Tara

6. No, it's not. It's exciting! It's fun!   Claudia / Mike / Tara

C What do they say? Watch the video. Write the words you hear to complete the conversations.

Tara:	This is my favorite game. Ready?
Claudia:	OK. But it is so (1)__crowded__. And this game is so boring!
Takeshi:	No, it isn't. It's (2)_____.
Mike:	And (3)_____!
Tara:	Here we go! What (4)_____ is it? It's big. It's really interesting.

. . . .

Roberto:	OK. What (5)_____ is it? It's in South America. It's a (6)_____ city, and my favorite person is from there.
Tara:	(7)_____'s your favorite person, Roberto?
Mike:	Ooh! (8)_____ are you from? Are you from São Paulo? Brasilia?

. . . .

Sun-hee:	Yay! My turn! What city is it? It's (9)_____ . . . and cheap. It's noisy . . . and (10)_____. It's modern, but some places are (11)_____.
All:	Huh? What?
Sun-hee:	OK. It's in the U.S. It's crowded. People from all over the world live there — Mexicans, Koreans, Brazilians, (12)_____ . . .

4 After You Watch

A Look at the conversation from the video in the box below. Study the expressions in red. Then match the expressions with the definitions.

Useful Expressions

Claudia: I know. It's **right here**. It's New York!

Sun-hee: You're correct.

Claudia: Yay! My turn!

Mike: Uh-uh! **Wait a minute!** "This game is so boring!"

Claudia: No, it's not. It's exciting! It's fun! **Come on**, Mike!

1. Something you say when you are surprised ___Wait a minute!_____

2. (In) this place _____

3. Something you say when you want people to do something _____

4. Something you say when you are excited and happy _____

B Now, complete the conversations below with the expressions from A.

1. A: Rio de Janeiro is the capital of Brazil.
   B: _____! No, it's not! It's Brasilia.

2. A: Russell Crowe is on TV tonight
   B: _____! He's my favorite actor!

3. A: _____. We're late for the movie!
   B: OK. I'm coming!

4. A: Where are you from?
   B: _____ in the U.S. I'm from Chicago.

Language Link: Question words *Who* and *Where*

who asks about people	*who's* = who is
where asks about places	*where's* = where is

Where *are you from?*

 In the video, the characters use *who* and *where* to play a game. Study the box. Then complete the conversation with *who* or *where*.

Nancy: Hello, Richard?

Richard: Yes. (1)___Who___ is this, please?

Nancy: Richard! It's me, Nancy.

Richard: Nancy! (2)_____ are you?

Nancy: I'm in France!

Richard: France? (3)_____ in France?

Nancy: In Paris. It's a beautiful city.

Richard: (4)_____ with you?

Nancy: My friend Paula.

Richard: (5)_____ is she from?

Nancy: She's from New York!

 Complete the story summary. Use the words in the box.

boring	difficult	answers	~~play~~	beautiful	from	fun	country

The characters (1)___play___ a game called "Where is it?" Claudia says the game is (2)_____ but she plays anyway. First, Tara asks a question about a (3)_____. Then Roberto asks a question about a city he thinks is (4)_____. He says, "My favorite person is (5)_____ there." Next Sun-hee gives a (6)_____ hint. Claudia (7)_____ it and it's her turn. Then she thinks the "boring" game is (8)_____!

Countries and Nationalities

Global Viewpoints | Where I'm From

1 Before You Watch

Here are some words you will hear in the interviews about "Where I'm From." Use the words to complete the sentences.

capital   mix   pretty

1. Miranda is a _____ girl.

2. Paris is the _____ of France.

3. New York is a _____ of many nationalities.

2 While You Watch

A Where are these people from? Watch the interviews and match the names with the cities.

1. Kumiko ___f___   a. Belo Horizonte

2. Jonathan ____   b. Dakar

3. Paula ____   c. Guatemala City

4. Dayanne ____   d. Paramus

5. Dennis ____   e. Manila

6. Calvin ____   f. ~~Tokyo~~

7. Woo Sung ____   g. Ulsan

8. Agnes ____   h. São Paulo

*Tokyo is a big city. There are **lots** of people.*

Real English

You can use **lots** or **a lot** to mean a large amount or number.

B Watch the interviews about "Where I'm From" again. What do the people say about these places? Check (✓) the words you hear.

1. Tokyo, Japan   ☐ big   ☐ modern   ☐ noisy   ☐ crowded

2. Guatemala City, Guatemala ☐ old   ☐ modern   ☐ noisy   ☐ interesting

3. São Paulo, Brazil   ☐ pretty   ☐ cheap   ☐ big   ☐ noisy

4. Manila, Philippines   ☐ crowded   ☐ pretty   ☐ old   ☐ new

5. Paramus, New Jersey   ☐ big   ☐ expensive   ☐ beautiful   ☐ modern

6. Dakar, Senegal   ☐ small   ☐ interesting ☐ old   ☐ new

1 Before You Watch

Here are some cities people talk about in the interviews about "Favorite Cities." Match the cities with the countries.

1. Singapore _e_

2. Boston, Massachusetts ___

3. Mexico City ___

4. Barcelona ___

5. Sydney ___

a. the U.S.

b. Mexico

c. Australia

d. Spain

e. ~~Singapore~~

2 While You Watch

What cities do these people like? Watch the interviews and circle the answers.

1. Brad's favorite city is in France /(Spain.)

2. Vanessa and Woo Sung like Boston / New York.

3. José Luis says Mexico City is big, noisy, and crowded / beautiful.

4. Calum's favorite city is Singapore / Hong Kong.

5. Kumiko thinks Australians / Americans are very kind.

6. Jonathan's favorite city is Boston / New York.

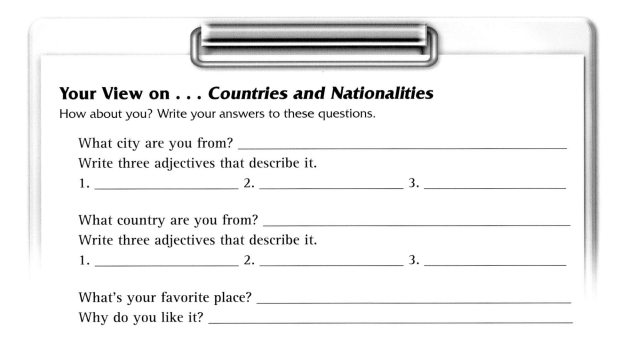

Your View on . . . *Countries and Nationalities*

How about you? Write your answers to these questions.

What city are you from? _____

Write three adjectives that describe it.

1. _____ 2. _____ 3. _____

What country are you from? _____

Write three adjectives that describe it.

1. _____ 2. _____ 3. _____

What's your favorite place? _____

Why do you like it? _____

3 Interesting Products
City Living | A Cool Gift

1 Preview

A In this episode, Sun-hee and Mike buy Tara a birthday present.

Here's a cool gift.

Sun-hee and Mike shop for Tara's gift.

Hi. May I help you?

Sun-hee and Mike go into an electronics store.

These TVs are great.

The salesman tells Sun-hee about different items.

Ooh...

Then Mike sees something interesting.

B Look at the photos above. Then complete the sentences with *a*, *b*, or *c*.

1. _____ finds a gift for Tara in the window.

    a. Mike   b. A salesman   c. Sun-hee

2. Sun-hee and Mike go into _____.

    a. a department store   b. a shoe store   c. an electronics store

3. The salesman tells Sun-hee the TVs are _____.

    a. expensive   b. good   c. big

4. Mike thinks another item in the store is _____.

    a. cool   b. boring   c. expensive

A Here are some words you will hear in the video. Write the correct word or words under each picture.

CD player   digital camera   DVD player   MP3 player

radio   ~~stereo (system)~~   speaker   karaoke (machine)

1. stereo system

2. _____

3. _____

4. _____

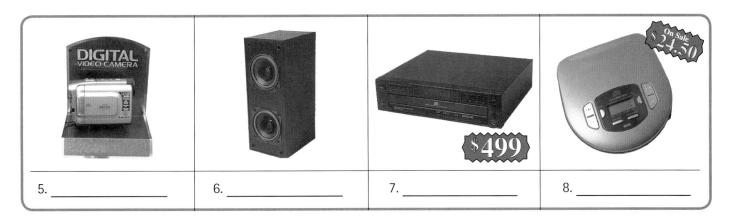

5. _____

6. _____

7. _____

8. _____

B Look at the pictures in **A** again. Circle the correct word in the statements below.

1. The stereo system is (fantastic) / terrible.

2. The CD player is expensive / inexpensive.

3. The MP3 player is lightweight / heavy.

4. The digital camera is old / new.

5. The DVD player is cheap / expensive.

3 While You Watch

 A What happens? Watch the video. Number the pictures from 1 to 5 to put them in order.

This is so cool!

Only Tara's gift, huh?

This DVD player really is a great gift.

Gee, that's expensive.

 B What's the story? Watch the video again. Check (✓) the sentences that are true. Then correct the false sentences.

1. ___✓___ Sun-hee sees a DVD player in a store window.

2. _____ Sun-hee wants to buy a birthday gift for Tara.

3. _____ The DVD player is $179.

4. _____ Mike thinks the DVD player is inexpensive.

5. _____ Mike and Sun-hee buy the DVD player.

6. _____ Sun-hee asks the salesman about digital cameras.

7. _____ Mike thinks the stereo is inexpensive.

8. _____ Sun-hee and Mike buy only Tara's gift.

What do they say? Watch the video. Write the words you hear to complete the conversations.

Gee, *that's expensive.*

Mike uses **gee** to express surprise and concern.

Salesman: Hi! May I help you?

Mike: Yes. Is (1)____this____ a good DVD player?

Salesman: Oh yes. It's a very (2)_____ DVD player and it's

(3)_____. It's only a hundred and twenty-nine dollars.

· ·

Salesman: This DVD (4)_____ really is a great gift. It's inexpensive and it's

(5)_____.

Sun-hee: Yeah, it is. Oh. And (6)_____ TVs are great, too.

Salesman: Oh, (7)_____ TVs are great. And this one has an (8)_____ rating.

· ·

Mike: Sun-hee! These speakers are (9)_____! My old speakers are

(10)_____, and these are really (11)_____! And this

stereo is really (12)_____!

A Study the expressions from the video in the box below. Then use the expressions to complete the conversations. Use each expression only once.

Useful Expressions

I don't know.

May I help you?

~~You're welcome.~~

Thank you so much.

We'll take it.

1. A: Thank you!
   B: _You're welcome._

2. A: _____
   B: Yes, please.

3. A: This TV is only $189.
   B: _____
   A: Great!

4. A: How much is that?
   B: _____
   A: Let's ask.

5. A: Here you are!
   B: _____
   A: My pleasure.

B Number the sentences from 1 to 5 to put the conversation in order.

_____ It's only $99.

_____ Great!

__1__ May I help you?

_____ That's cheap! I'll take it!

_____ Yes, please. How much is this camera?

Language Link: Adjectives and nouns

	be + adjective	Adjective + noun
singular	This camera is nice.	This is a nice camera.
plural	These cameras **are** nice.	These are nice cameras.

 In the video, the salesman uses an adjective plus a noun to talk about the DVD player. Study the box. Then unscramble the following words to make sentences.

1. cameras / Those / Japanese / are

   Those are Japanese cameras.

2. an / A / is/ gift / TV / expensive

   _____

3. fantastic / is / That / stereo

   _____

4. speakers / big / are / These

   _____

5. are / These / CD players / terrible

   _____

 Complete the story summary. Use the words in the box.

| ~~electronics~~ | expensive | birthday | gift | MP3 player | stereo | TV's | DVD player |

   Sun-hee and Mike walk by an (1) electronics store. Sun-hee sees a (2)_____ in the store window. She wants to buy it for Tara's (3)_____. They go into the store to buy Tara's gift. Mike thinks the DVD player is (4)_____. Sun-hee looks at some (5)_____. Mike looks at a (6)_____. It has a radio, a CD player, an (7)_____, and karaoke. Sun-hee and Mike buy Tara's (8)_____ and a lot of other things, too!

Interesting Products

Global Viewpoints | Personal Items

---

1 Before You Watch

Here are some words you will hear in the interviews about "Personal Items." Write the correct word or words under each picture.

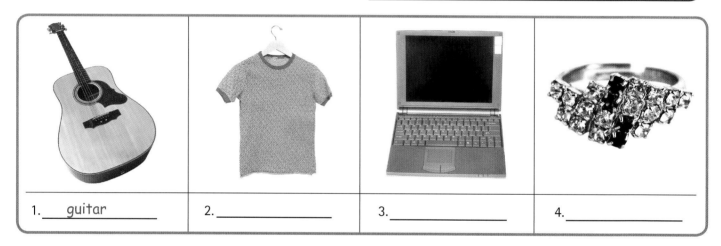

1. ___guitar___
2. _____
3. _____
4. _____

---

2 While You Watch

What do these people talk about? Watch the interviews and check (✓) the personal item(s) each person names.

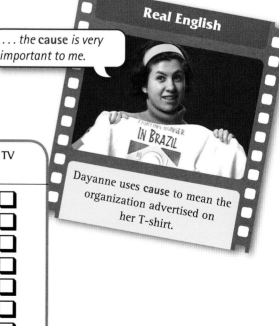

Real English

. . . the cause is very important to me.

Dayanne uses **cause** to mean the organization advertised on her T-shirt.

	CD player	laptop/ computer	guitar	ring	stereo	T-shirt	TV
1. Dennis	✓	☐	☐	☐	☐	☐	☐
2. Agnes	☐	☐	☐	☐	☐	☐	☐
3. Woo Sung	☐	☐	☐	☐	☐	☐	☐
4. Brad	☐	☐	☐	☐	☐	☐	☐
5. Dayanne	☐	☐	☐	☐	☐	☐	☐
6. Alejandra	☐	☐	☐	☐	☐	☐	☐
7. Hana	☐	☐	☐	☐	☐	☐	☐

1 Before You Watch

You will hear the words below in the interviews about "Favorite Gifts."
Write each word once to answer the questions.

chocolate

earrings

cameras

1. What do people wear?

_____

2. What do people eat?

_____

3. What takes photos?

_____

2 While You Watch

What gifts do these people like? Watch the interviews and circle the correct answers.

1. What is Catherine's favorite gift?   chocolate / earrings / a camera
2. What is Agnes's favorite gift?   chocolate / earrings / a camera
3. What is Alejandra's favorite gift?   chocolate / earrings / a camera

Your View on . . . *Interesting Products*
How about you? Answer the questions below.

1. What electronic items do you have in your home? Make a list.

   _____   _____

   _____   _____

2. What is your favorite personal item? Why?

   _____

3. What is your favorite gift? Why?

   _____

4 Activities and Interests

City Living | What are you doing—now?

1 Preview

 A In this episode, Claudia gets a new picture phone.

Here I am!

Claudia calls Tara and sends a picture from her new picture phone.

No, I'm not studying. I'm exercising now.

Tara is busy, but Claudia calls her again.

Oh, hi Claudia.

Sun-hee and Tara are watching TV, and the phone rings.

Then Sun-hee and Tara get a very interesting photo from Claudia.

B Look at the photos above. Then complete the sentences with *a*, *b*, or *c*.

1. Claudia's cell phone is _____.

    a. old   b. new   c. terrible

2. When Claudia calls a second time, Tara is _____.

    a. studying   b. exercising   c. not exercising

3. When Sun-hee answers the phone, Tara _____.

    a. doesn't want to talk b. is happy   c. is sleeping

4. Claudia sends Tara and Sun-hee _____.

    a. a message   b. her phone number   c. a picture

2 Before You Watch

 A Here are some words you will hear in the video. Use the words to complete the sentences.

cooking	shopping	sleeping	studying
~~taking~~	talking	waiting	watching

1. They're ___taking___ a class.

2. They're _____ a movie.

3. He's _____ on the phone.

4. He's _____ .

5. She's _____ for a friend.

6. They're _____ .

7. She's _____ .

8. He's _____ .

 B Here are some more words you will hear in the video. Use the words to complete the sentences.

1. I'm taking an English class this _semester_ .

2. He's not ugly. He's _____!

3. She likes to eat Brazilian _____.

4. _____ people have many things to do.

5. He has a _____ with a pretty girl on Saturday night.

6. This _____ is by Picasso.

7. Marina and I are in the same class. She's my _____.

busy	classmate	cute	date
food	painting	~~semester~~	

City Living **27**

3 While You Watch

A What's the story? Watch the video. Check (✓) the sentences that are true. Then correct the false sentences.

1. ___✓___ Claudia calls Tara on her cell phone.

2. _____ Tara is sleeping when Claudia calls.

3. _____ Claudia tells Tara she has a date with Miguel.

4. _____ Claudia calls Tara again and says she is waiting for Roberto.

5. _____ Claudia calls Sun-hee and Tara from the Cat Club.

6. _____ Claudia sends a picture of Roberto from the Cat Club.

7. _____ Sun-hee and Tara are not excited to meet Miguel.

B What are they saying? Watch the video again. Match the sentences with the pictures.

Here he is now!

Well, have fun.

~~I'm shopping right now.~~

They're dancing.

He's pretty cute.

1. Claudia: _I'm shopping right now._

2. Tara: _____

_____

3. Claudia: _____

_____

4. Claudia: _____

_____

5. Sun-hee: _____

_____

What do they say? Watch the video. Write the words you hear to complete the conversations.

Tara: So, what are you doing?

Claudia: (1)_____Talking_____ on the phone. I'm (2)_____ right now. And I have a

(3)_____ with Roberto for dinner at his house later. He's (4)_____ an Italian cooking class.

· ·

Claudia: Are you (5)_____?

Tara: No, I'm not (6)_____. I'm (7)_____ now.

Claudia: I'm (8)_____ for Roberto. Hey! Here he is now.

· ·

Claudia: What are you (9)_____?

Sun-hee: Oh, just (10)_____ TV.

Claudia: Oh, where's Tara?

Sun-hee: Tara? Uh . . . she's (11)_____.

Claudia: Really? Gee, that's too bad.

Sun-hee: Why? What are you up to?

Claudia: Roberto and I are out (12)_____.

4 After You Watch

 A Study the expressions from the video in the box below. Then match each expression with the sentence that has the same meaning.

> **Useful Expressions**
>
> That's cool.
>
> ~~What are you up to?~~
>
> That's too bad.
>
> Got to go!

1. What are you doing? _What are you up to?_ _____

2. I'm leaving now. _____

3. That's nice. _____

4. I'm sorry. _____

B Now, complete the conversation. Use the expressions from A.

Ben:	Hi, Ken. This is Ben.
Ken:	Hi, Ben, (1)____ _What are you up to?_ ____
Ben:	I'm waiting for Eva. We're going to a movie.
Ken:	(2)_____ What movie are you seeing?
Ben:	The new one with Tom Cruise. What are you doing?
Ken:	I'm studying. I'm not doing well in my classes.
Ben:	(3)_____
Ken:	Yeah, it is. I want to see that movie.
Ben:	Sorry. Well, here's Eva now. (4)_____

Language Link: Present continuous

Statements	Negative Forms	*Wh-* questions	*Yes/No* questions
I am talking.	I am not talking.	What are you doing?	Are you talking?
He/She/It is working.	He/She/It is not working.	What is he doing?	Is he working?
We are cooking.	We are not cooking.	What is he watching?	Is she studying?
They are dancing.	They are not dancing.	What are they doing?	Are they dancing?

I'm calling *you on my new cell phone!*

C In the video, Claudia uses the present continuous to say what she is doing. Study the box. Then use the present continuous to complete the phone conversation.

Jane: Hello?

Rebecca: Hey, Jane. It's Rebecca. What (you / do) (1)__are you doing__?

           (you / watch) (2)_____ TV?

Jane: No, (I / not / watch) (3)_____ TV. (I / study) (4)_____ .

Rebecca: What (you / study) (5)_____ ?

Jane: History. (I / not / do) (6)_____ well in my history class. Where are you?

Rebecca: In an electronics store. I'm with Paul. (We / shop) (7)_____ for a DVD player.

D Complete the story summary. Use the words in the box.

> exercising   watching TV   classmate   dancing   date   picture   ~~studying~~   waiting

Claudia calls Tara on her new cell phone. Tara is (1)__studying__. Claudia says, "I have a (2)_____ with Roberto." Later, Claudia calls Tara again. Tara is (3)_____. Claudia is (4)_____ for Roberto. He arrives and Claudia takes his (5)_____ with her cell phone. That evening, Tara and Sun-hee are (6)_____. Claudia calls and says, "Roberto and I are out (7)_____. We're at the Cat Club with Roberto's (8)_____ Miguel." When Tara and Sun-hee see Miguel's picture, they leave for the Cat Club!

Activities and Interests

Global Viewpoints | At School

1 Before You Watch

 A Here are two words you will hear in the interviews about "At School." Write the correct word under each picture.

(painter)   (sculptor)

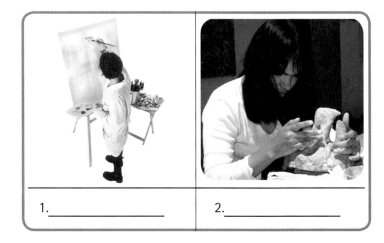

1. _____   2. _____

B Here are some school subjects people mention in the interviews. Write the subjects in the chart.

~~accounting information systems~~	American history	sculpting	business
music recording	Chinese literature	economics	French
health and wellness	communications	painting	education
business law	music history	anthropology	sociology

Art and Music	Business and Economics
_____	accounting information systems
_____	_____
_____	_____
_____	_____

Languages and Literature	Other
_____	_____
_____	_____
_____	_____
	_____
	_____
	_____

2 While You Watch

What classes are these people taking? Watch the interviews and match the names with the classes.

1. Jackie ___b___
2. Woo Sung _____
3. Dave _____
4. Brad _____
5. Calvin _____
6. Hana _____
7. Agnes _____

a. business law and accounting information systems

b. ~~French 101, American history, Chinese literature, and education~~

c. communications and music

d. not taking any classes; writing final paper

e. art history, music history, health and wellness, and music recording

f. anthropology, economics, sociology, and history

g. painting and sculpting

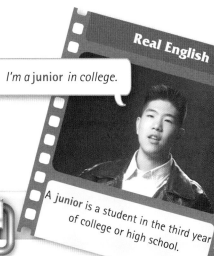

Real English

I'm a junior in college.

A junior is a student in the third year of college or high school.

Your View on . . . *Activities and Interests*
How about you? Answer the questions below.

1. Do you have a cell phone? What do you think of cell phones?

   _____

2. Do you like talking on the phone? Who do you call most often?

   _____

3. Are you taking classes right now? What classes are you doing well in?

   _____

4. What's your favorite subject?

   _____

5 Food

City Living | Takeshi's Food Video

1 Preview

 A In this episode, Takeshi makes a video about eating habits.

So you push here, OK?

Takeshi teaches Mike how to use a video camera.

Hi guys!

Claudia and Tara arrive at the apartment.

For breakfast I have fruit . . .

Takeshi interviews Claudia and Tara about their eating habits.

But then Mike makes a big mistake!

B Look at the photos above. Then complete the sentences with *a*, *b*, or *c*.

1. Where is Takeshi making the video? _____

   a. at school   b. in his apartment   c. on the street

2. What does Mike learn how to do? _____

   a. use a camera   b. answer the door   c. interview people

3. Who does Takeshi ask questions about food? _____

   a. Claudia and Mike   b. Mike and Tara   c. Claudia and Tara

4. At what meal does Claudia have fruit? _____

   a. dinner   b. breakfast   c. snacks

2 Before You Watch

A Here are some words you will hear in the video. Match the words with the pictures.

1. _c_ bacon
2. ___ beans
3. ___ eggs
4. ___ fruit
5. ___ mushrooms
6. ___ orange juice
7. ___ sausage
8. ___ toast
9. ___ tomatoes
10. ___ yogurt

B Here are some more words you will hear in the video. Write the correct word or words under each picture.

chicken	salad	steak	tea
(potato) chips	~~coffee~~	ice cream	

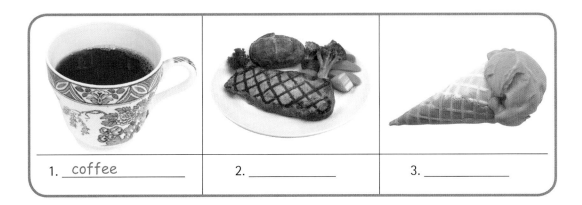

1. __coffee__
2. _____
3. _____

4. _____
5. _____
6. _____
7. _____

3 While You Watch

 A What do you learn about the characters? Watch the video. Circle the answers.

1. Takeshi is taking a <u>cooking</u> / (film) class.

2. Claudia has fruit, yogurt, and <u>tea / orange juice</u> for breakfast.

3. Claudia <u>drinks / doesn't drink</u> coffee.

4. Tara eats a <u>big / small</u> breakfast.

5. Tara usually has <u>sausage / a salad</u> for lunch.

6. Tara works at a <u>restaurant / movie theater</u>.

7. <u>Tara / Claudia</u> sometimes has chicken for dinner.

8. Claudia doesn't eat <u>steak / junk food</u>.

B What are they saying? Watch the video again. Match the sentences with the pictures.

> It's a videotape.
>
> It has eggs, bacon, sausage . . .
>
> What about all that junk food you eat?
>
> I'm a vegetarian.
>
> ~~We're making a video . . .~~

1. Takeshi: <u>We're making a video . . .</u>

2. Tara: _____

3. Claudia: _____

4. Tara: _____

5. Mike: _____

What do they say? Watch the video. Write the words you hear to complete the conversations.

Real English

Yep, everything's set.

People sometimes use everything's set to mean everything is ready.

Claudia: For breakfast I (1)_____have_____ fruit, yogurt, and orange juice.

Takeshi: Hmm, that's pretty healthy. (2)_____ you have any coffee or tea?

Claudia: Nope. I don't (3)_____ coffee. I (4)_____ like the caffeine.

. . . .

Takeshi: Now, how about you, Tara? Do you (5)_____ a healthy breakfast, too?

Claudia: Ha! She (6)_____ not healthy! She (7)_____ a really big English

breakfast every day.

Tara: (8)_____ every day!

Takeshi: Well, what's an English breakfast?

Tara: Well, it (9)_____ eggs, bacon, sausage, tomatoes, mushrooms, beans, toast . . .

. . . .

Takeshi: How about you, Claudia? Do you (10)_____ steak?

Claudia: No, I don't (11)_____ steak. I'm a vegetarian.

Takeshi: Wow, you (12)_____ healthy, aren't you!

A Study the expressions from the video in the box below. Then use the expressions to complete the conversations. Use each expression only once.

> **Useful Expressions**
>
> How about you?
>
> ~~How's (school) going?~~
>
> Me, too.
>
> No problem!
>
> Sounds good.

1. A: <u>How's school going?</u>
   B: Pretty well. I like my classes.

2. A: I like coffee.
   _____
   B: No, I don't like coffee.

3. A: I really like ice cream.
   B: _____

4. A: I'll call you later, OK?
   B: _____

5. A: Can you help me, please?
   B: _____

B Number the sentences 1 to 5 to put the conversation in order.

_____ Sounds good. Can you give me a call?

_____ I'm fine, thanks. Hey, let's have dinner next week!

___1___ Hi, Patrick! How are you?

_____ I'm great, Jen. How about you?

_____ No problem. Got to go!

Language Link: Simple present

| I
You
We
They | like
don't like | coffee. | He
She | likes
doesn't like | coffee. |

 In the video, Claudia uses the simple present to say what she has for breakfast. Study the box. Then use the simple present to complete the sentences.

For breakfast I have fruit, yogurt, and orange juice.

1. My sister (not / eat) ___doesn't eat___ meat. She's a vegetarian.

2. I (like) _____ chicken.

3. My friends (not / like) _____ steak.

4. People in my country (have) _____ tea for breakfast.

5. Edgar (drink) _____ a lot of coffee.

6. He (not / drink) _____ tea.

7. Linda (exercise) _____ every day.

D **Complete the story summary. Use the words in the box.**

| arrive | answers | ~~helps~~ | interviews | start | stops | answer | sees |

Takeshi is making a video for his film class, so Mike

(1)___helps___ him. Claudia and Tara (2)_____

at the apartment. Mike (3)_____ the door. Takeshi

(4)_____ Claudia and Tara about their eating habits.

They (5)_____ his questions and (6)_____ to

argue. Takeshi (7)_____ the interview and then he

(8)_____ the videotape on a chair. Mike says, "Cut!"

when he understands his mistake.

Food

Global Viewpoints | Meals

1 Before You Watch

Here are some words and phrases you will hear in the interviews about "Meals." Write the correct word or phrase under each picture.

cereal	~~corn~~	fish	a piece of toast
pasta	rice	milk	a turkey sandwich

1. corn   2. _____   3. _____   4. _____

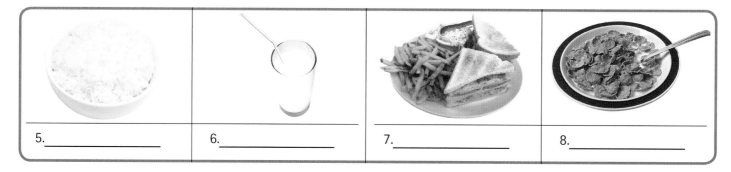

5. _____   6. _____   7. _____   8. _____

2 While You Watch

What do these people eat? Watch the interviews and circle *True* or *False*. Then correct the false sentences.

a piece of toast

1. Kumiko has ~~cereal~~ and coffee for breakfast.   True / (False)
2. Alejandra has a healthy breakfast.   True / False
3. Woo Sung has a big breakfast.   True / False
4. Jonathan makes a sandwich for lunch.   True / False
5. Agnes has rice with beans.   True / False
6. Woo Sung eats a sandwich and soup for lunch.   True / False
7. Agnes doesn't like pasta.   True / False
8. Calvin doesn't usually eat dinner.   True / False

Global Viewpoints | Likes and Dislikes

1 Before You Watch

You will hear the words *smell, taste,* and *texture* in the interviews about "Likes and Dislikes." Read the sample sentences, then circle the correct word to complete each definition.

1. Do you like the **smell** of coffee?
2. I like the **taste** of chocolate.
3. Yogurt has a creamy **texture**.

You notice a **smell** with your <u>nose / ears</u>.
You notice a **taste** with your <u>eyes / mouth</u>.
You notice a food's **texture** with your <u>tongue / nose</u>.

2 While You Watch

What do these people say? Watch the interviews and match the names with the sentences.

1. Dennis <u>c</u>
2. Denise ___
3. Alejandra ___
4. Kumiko ___
5. Kevin ___
6. Jonathan ___
7. Jackie ___
8. Catherine ___

a. I don't eat meat because I don't like it.
b. My favorite food is *quesadilla de mole*.
c. ~~I love to eat and I love to cook.~~
d. My favorite food is Japanese sushi.
e. I don't really have a favorite food.
f. I like a bowl of white rice and *kimchi*.
g. My son Ricardo loves hamburgers.
h. I don't like beans. I don't like the taste and the texture.

Real English

I like mostly everything.

People sometimes use *mostly* to mean "almost" in informal conversation.

Your View on . . . *Food*
How about you? Answer the questions below.

1. What do you have for breakfast? For lunch? For dinner?

   _____

2. What is your favorite food?

   _____

3. What food(s) do you dislike?

   _____

4. What foods do you think are healthy? Unhealthy?

   _____

6 My Family

City Living | Roberto's Family Picture

1 Preview

A In this episode, Roberto tells Claudia about his family.

She's my sister Louisa's daughter.

Roberto tells Claudia about his niece who is visiting.

It's Rita's picture of our family.

Roberto shows Claudia his niece's drawing.

I'm Claudia.

Nice to meet you.

Rita comes in while Roberto is talking about his family.

Rita has a surprising viewpoint about her uncle Roberto.

B Look at the photos above. Then complete the sentences with *a*, *b*, or *c*.

1. Rita is Roberto's _____.

   a. daughter   b. sister   c. niece

2. Rita draws a picture of _____.

   a. herself   b. her family   c. Claudia

3. Roberto has a _____ family.

   a. big   b. quiet   c. small

4. Roberto _____ Claudia about his family.

   a. asks   b. tells   c. doesn't talk to

2 Before You Watch

A Here are some words you will hear in the video. Match the words with the people in the pictures.

Jenny's . . .
1. ~~father (dad)~~
2. mother (mom)
3. brother

Enrico's . . .
4. wife
5. son
6. daughter

Laura's . . .
7. husband
8. sister

Jenny	Enrico	Laura

B Here are some more words you will hear in the video. Look at the family tree and use the words to complete the sentences below.

aunt   cousin   niece   single parent   ~~uncle~~

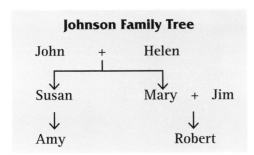

Johnson Family Tree

John   +   Helen

Susan   Mary + Jim

Amy   Robert

1. Jim is Amy's ___uncle___ .

2. Susan is Robert's _____ .

3. Amy is Robert's _____ .

4. Amy is Mary's _____ .

5. Susan is a _____ .

A What happens? Watch the video. Number the pictures from 1 to 5 to put them in order.

 B What's the story? Watch the video again. Check (✓) the sentences that are true. Then correct the false sentences.

1. ___✓___ Rita is Roberto's niece.

2. _____ Rita lives in New York.

3. _____ Raquel is Roberto's sister.

4. _____ Silvio is Roberto's uncle.

5. _____ Marco is Roberto's brother.

6. _____ Emilio and Olivia are Roberto's cousins.

7. _____ Emilio is thirty-three.

8. _____ Olivia is twenty-six.

What do they say? Watch the video. Write the words you hear to complete the conversations.

Real English

That's Grampa *Martinez.*

Grampa is a nickname for grandfather.

Claudia: Hey, what's that?

Roberto: It's (1)_____Rita's_____ picture of (2)_____ family.

Claudia: Oh, it's beautiful. And wow! (3)_____ many people are there in

(4)_____family?

Roberto: A lot! I have a really big family.

. . . .

Claudia: Who's that?

Roberto: This is (5)_____ mother, Raquel, and this is my (6)_____, Silvio.

And this is my (7)_____ Louisa, Rita's mom, and (8)_____

husband, Rico.

. . . .

Claudia: OK . . . and these two? What are (9)_____ names?

Roberto: That's Marco, my older (10)_____, and this is Tomás, (11)_____

son. He's a single (12)_____.

A Look at the conversations from the video in the box below. Study the expressions in red. Then match the expressions with the definitions.

> ### Useful Expressions
>
> **Claudia:** Hey, Roberto! How's it going?
>
> **Roberto:** Well, life's definitely not boring. My little niece Rita is visiting from Los Angeles. She's sleeping right now, but wow! Busy, busy, busy!
>
> **Claudia:** How nice! How old is she?
>
> ***
>
> **Claudia:** They look pretty cool. How old are they?
>
> **Roberto:** Let's see, Emilio is twenty-three, and Olivia is twenty-six.

1. Something you say to show excitement, surprise, etc. _____Wow!_____

2. Something you say when you need time to think of an answer _____

3. Something you say when you greet people _____

4. Something you say when someone tells you some good news _____

B Now, complete the conversations below with the expressions from A.

1. A: I have ten brothers and sisters.
   B: _____Wow!_____

2. A: _____
   B: Pretty good, but I'm really busy.

3. A: Where's Angela from?
   B: _____ I think she's from Peru.

4. A: My sister's visiting from London.
   B: _____

Language Link: Possessives

singular noun + 's	Joe is **Mary's** brother. **Peter's** wife is Jane.	Joe is **her** brother. **His** wife is Jane.
plural noun + '	My **parents'** apartment is small.	**Their** apartment is small.
irregular plural noun + 's	The **children's** names are Joe and Emily.	**Their** names are Joe and Emily.

**In the video, Roberto uses a possessive to talk about his niece.
Study the box. Then add 's or ' to complete the sentences.**

She's my sister Louisa's daughter.

1. Alex is (Carol)____*Carol's*____ brother.

2. (Kenji) _____ sister lives in Tokyo.

3. Who is the (children) _____ father?

4. The (baby) _____ mother is beautiful.

5. (Lisa) _____ mother is an actress.

6. Both (families) _____ houses were really nice.

Complete the story summary. Use the words in the box.

Roberto's	Who's	old	~~his~~	How many	How	Her	their

    Claudia visits Roberto at (1)_____*his*_____ apartment.

(2)_____ niece is visiting from Los Angeles.

(3)_____ name is Rita. Roberto shows Claudia Rita's

picture of (4)_____ family. Claudia asks questions

such as "(5)_____ people are there in your family?"

and "(6)_____ that?" Rita joins them and Claudia

asks "(7)_____ old is Grampa Martinez?" Rita

answers, "I don't know, but he's really (8)_____,

just like Uncle Roberto."

My Family

Global Viewpoints | My Family

1 Before You Watch

Here are some words you will hear in the interviews about "My Family." Read what Tereza says about her family. Fill in the blanks. Use the words in the box.

nephew   older   younger

Hi! My name is Tereza. I'm 21 years old. I have two sisters, Inés and Juana. Inés, my (1)_____ sister, is 19. Joana, my (2)_____ sister, is 28. Nelson is my (3)_____. He's my sister Joana's son.

2 While You Watch

Watch the interviews and circle the correct answers.

1. Hana's _____ name is Helen.

   a. mother's   b. sister's   c. aunt's

2. Yelena has a _____.

   a. niece   b. sister   c. nephew

3. Alejandra has an older _____.

   a. cousin   b. sister   c. brother

4. José Luis has _____ sisters.

   a. two   b. three   c. four

5. Agnes has twelve _____.

   a. brothers and sisters   b. uncles and aunts   c. cousins

6. Brad has _____ family.

   a. no   b. a small   c. a big

1 Before You Watch

You will hear the words below in the interviews in "All about Me." Use the words below to complete the sentences. Use each word only once.

> fiancé   cute   ~~currently~~
> married   smart

1. <u>Currently</u> means "now" or "at this time."

2. _____ people are attractive and easy to like.

3. A woman's _____ is her future husband.

4. Another word for intelligent is _____.

5. A _____ person has a husband or wife.

2 While You Watch

Watch the interviews and check (✓) the sentences that are true. Then correct the false sentences.

1. ___✓___ Nick is 23 years old.

2. _____ Agnes is single.

3. _____ Denise's son is ten years old.

4. _____ Alejandra has two children.

5. _____ Natalie is a single mother.

6. _____ Yelena doesn't have any children.

7. _____ Kumiko is single.

8. _____ Kevin is married.

9. _____ Catherine has a fiancé.

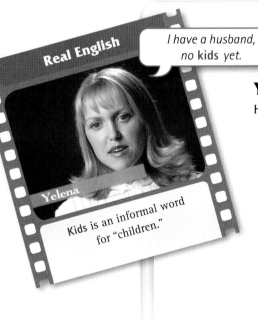

Real English

I have a husband, no kids yet.

Yelena

Kids is an informal word for "children."

Your View on . . . *My Family*

How about you? Answer the questions below.

1. How many people are there in your family?

   _____

2. What are your mother's and father's names?

   _____

3. Do you have any aunts, uncles, or cousins? How old are they? What are their names?

   _____

4. Do you like big families? Why or why not?

   _____

1 Preview

A In this episode, Mike talks about his daily schedule.

Takeshi comes home and finds Mike watching TV . . . again!

Mike, you really need a job.

Takeshi gives Mike some advice.

Busy? You don't work. You don't go to school...

Mike says he's too busy for a job.

At 9:00 I have my yoga class

Mike tells Takeshi about his "busy" schedule.

Maria? Who's Maria?

Then Mike talks about a "special friend" he sees on Wednesday nights.

B Look at the photos above. Then circle the correct answers.

1. Takeshi thinks Mike <u>needs / doesn't need</u> a job.

2. Mike <u>wants / doesn't want</u> a job.

3. Mike <u>goes / doesn't go</u> to school.

4. Mike's schedule <u>does / doesn't</u> include exercise.

5. Takeshi <u>knows / doesn't know</u> Maria.

2 Before You Watch

A Here are some activities you will hear in the video. Match each activity with the correct picture.

a. go to the movies   c. have a yoga class   e. spend time with (family)   g. relax
b. go to school   d. meet (a person)   f. work out at the gym   h. work

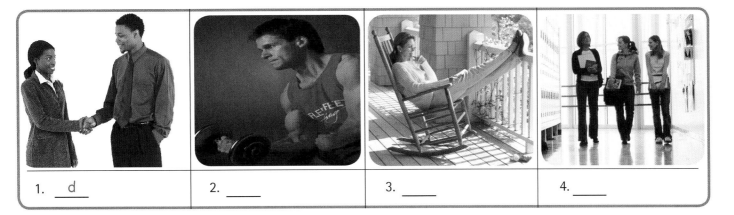

1. __d__   2. _____   3. _____   4. _____

5. _____   6. _____   7. _____   8. _____

B Here are some phrases you will hear in the video. Use the phrases to complete the paragraph. Use each phrase only once.

in the afternoon   in the morning   at night   at noon

What do I do every day? Well, I get up at 6:30 __in the morning__.

I leave for work at 7:00. _____, I go to a restaurant

for lunch. After lunch, I go back to work. I finish work at 3:30

_____. Then I go home and relax or spend time

with friends. I go to sleep at 11:00 _____.

A What happens? Watch the video. Number the pictures from 1 to 5 to put them in order.

B What do you learn about the characters? Watch the video again and circle the correct answers.

1. In the morning, Mike goes to work / works out at the gym.

2. In the afternoon he relaxes / goes shopping.

3. On Wednesday mornings he has a yoga class at nine / ten o'clock.

4. He has lunch at noon / one o'clock.

5. On Wednesday afternoons he has a film class / goes to the movies.

6. Maria lives / doesn't live in New York.

7. She is an actress / a news reporter.

8. On Wednesday nights Mike goes out with Maria / watches Maria on TV.

What do they say? Watch the video again. Write the words you hear to complete the conversations.

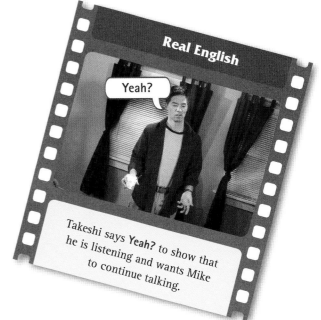

Yeah?

Takeshi says **Yeah?** to show that he is listening and wants Mike to continue talking.

Takeshi: What do you do all (1)_____day_____?

Mike: A lot of things.

Takeshi: Like what?

Mike: Well, in the (2)_____ I work out at the gym.

Takeshi: Yeah?

Mike: And then (3)_____ the afternoon I relax.

. . . .

Mike: Well, I'm (4)_____ today because I have a busy schedule tomorrow.

Takeshi: Oh, really?

Mike: Yeah. (5)_____ nine o'clock I have my yoga class. And then at (6)_____ I have lunch. Hey, don't laugh, it's an important meal. And then at (7)_____ I have my film class.

Takeshi: Mike, that's not a class. You go to the movies (8)_____ Wednesday afternoons.

. . . .

Takeshi: Wow. She sounds terrific. (9)_____ can I meet her?

Mike: Actually, right now. Here she is. She's on (10)_____ at 7:30 at (11)_____, but on (12)_____ she's on Channel four in the afternoon.

4 After You Watch

A Study the expressions from the video in the box below. Then use the expressions to complete the conversations. Use each expression only once.

> **Useful Expressions**
>
> Like what?
>
> What does he do?
>
> All the time!
>
> ~~Oh, really?~~
>
> You know,

1. A: My sister is on TV.
   B: <u>Oh, really?</u>

2. A: Your new boyfriend is cute!

   _____

   B: He's an actor.

3. A: How often do you watch that TV show "Dreams"?
   B: _____ I love it!

4. A: I have a new phone.
   B: Really? What kind of phone?
   A: _____ a cell phone!

5. A: I have so many things to do on Mondays!
   B: _____
   A: I go to school, I work and I have cooking class at night.

B Now, number the sentences 1 to 7 to put the conversation in order.

_____ Like what?

_____ No, he's not. He's an actor.

_____ Well, he's on *Kids*, *Free Zone* and *Action Hills*.

_____ Wow! I watch those shows all the time!

___1___ That's your brother Brad? Is he a singer?

_____ Oh, really? What kind of actor?

_____ You know, a movie actor. But he's on a lot of TV shows, too.

Language Link: Prepositions of time—*in*, *on*, and *at*			
It's **on** Monday. 　**on** Tuesday night. 　**on** the weekend.	*on* + day(s) of the week	It's **in** the morning. 　**in** the afternoon. 　**in** the evening.	*in* + time period of the day
It's **at** 8 o'clock. 　**at** 1:30. 　**at** noon.	*at* + specific time	It's **at** night.	(note the exception)

> *At 9 o'clock I have my yoga class.*

C In the video, Mike uses prepositions of time to talk about his schedule. Study the box. Then complete the sentences with *in*, *on*, or *at*.

1. My English class is _____*at*_____ 9:15 _____ the morning.

2. I like to watch TV _____ the weekend.

3. My favorite show is _____ Saturday _____ 7:00.

4. _____ Saturdays, I have a class _____ the afternoon and work _____ night.

5. Classes end _____ noon _____ Friday.

6. The concert starts _____ 5:30 _____ the evening.

D Complete the story summary. Use the words in the box.

at	busy	girlfriend	in	~~job~~	on	TV	has

Takeshi thinks Mike needs a (1)__*job*__. Mike says he's too (2)_____ for a job and tells Takeshi his schedule. On Wednesdays he (3)_____ a yoga class at 9:00 (4)_____ the morning. He has lunch (5)_____ noon, and at 4:45 he goes to the movies. He spends time with Maria (6)_____ Wednesday nights. She's an actress. She's not Mike's (7)_____, but he watches her all the time-on (8)_____!

Time

Global Viewpoints | Times and Schedules

1 Before You Watch

Here are some phrases you will hear in the interviews about "Times and Schedules." Write the correct phrase under each picture.

> practice piano   come back (home)   prepare dinner   go to sleep
> arrive at work   ~~wake up / get up~~   take a shower   leave for work

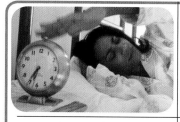

1. wake up / get up

2. _____

3. _____

4. _____

5. _____

6. _____

7. _____

8. _____

2 While You Watch

What do these people say? Watch the interviews and match the names with the sentences.

1. José Luis ___b___
2. Hana _____
3. Reda _____
4. Dave _____
5. Paula _____
6. Woo Sung _____
7. Catherine _____

a. I go to sleep at two A.M.
b. ~~I wake up early.~~
c. Around 7:30 I leave for work . . .
d. I like to wake up at nine o'clock . . .
e. I go to class from about ten to about five.
f. I don't get up early in the morning.
g. I get up at seven o'clock in the morning every day.

...and that's it *for the night.*

Real English

People sometimes say that's it to mean something is finished or over.

Global Viewpoints | Weekend Activities

1 Before You Watch

 You will hear the words below in the interviews about "Weekend Activities." Use the words or phrases to complete the sentences. Use each word only once.

| go to bed | books | party |

1. She has a lot of _____ about art and music.
2. Do you want to go to his birthday _____?
3. I _____ at 11:00 at night.

2 While You Watch

What do these people do on weekends? Watch the interviews and circle *Yes* or *No*.

1. Does José Luis go to parties?   Yes / No
2. Do Kumiko and her husband often go to restaurants?   Yes / No
3. Does Brad get up early on weekends?   Yes / No
4. Does Brad's girlfriend go to the gym on weekends?   Yes / No

Your View on . . . *Time*
How about you? Answer the questions below.

1. What are some things you do every day? Make a list. Include the times you do these things.

   _____ _____ _____
   _____ _____ _____

2. What do you usually do on weekends? Make a list.

   _____ _____ _____
   _____ _____ _____

3. What day(s) do you have a busy schedule? What do you do on those days?

   _____
   _____

8 Special Occasions
City Living | I love parades!

1 Preview

 A In this episode, Claudia, Roberto, Sun-hee, and Takeshi plan to see a parade.

The Puerto Rican Day Parade is my favorite!

Everyone is excited about the parade.

People sing, they dance...

Claudia tells the group about the day's events.

Well, the parade is 12:00 to about 3

Roberto talks about the celebration, too.

The group arrives at the parade location.

We're looking for the Puerto Rican Day Parade.

Roberto hears some bad news.

B Look at the photos above. Then complete the sentences with *a*, *b*, or *c*.

1. Roberto _____ the Puerto Rican Day Parade.

   a. likes   b. doesn't like   c. hates

2. Claudia says there is _____ at the celebration.

   a. singing and costumes   b. dancing and singing   c. music and games

3. The parade starts at _____.

   a. 3:00   b. 2:00   c. 12:00

4. The parade lasts about _____.

   a. two hours   b. three hours   c. twelve hours

5. Roberto wants to know _____ the parade is.

   a. what time   b. how long   c. where

2 Before You Watch

A You will hear some of these months in the video. Write the months in the correct order on the list.

December	February	October
~~January~~	June	August

Months of the Year

1. _January_   7. July
2. _____   8. _____
3. March   9. September
4. April   10. _____
5. May   11. November
6. _____   12. _____

B You will hear some dates in the video. Match the words with the numbers for the dates below.

1. October fifteenth _c_
2. June sixth ___
3. February twelfth ___
4. December seventeenth ___
5. July fourth ___

a. 12 / 17
b. 2 / 12
c. ~~10 / 15~~
d. 7 / 4
e. 6 / 6

C Here are some more words you will hear in the video. Use the words to complete the sentences below.

celebration	New Year's Day	hungry	Puerto Rican	~~parade~~	delicious

1. In the U.S., there is often a ___parade___ on the 4th of July.
2. People from Puerto Rico are _____.
3. _____ people need to eat food.
4. Many people celebrate _____ on January 1st.
5. This pizza is really _____!
6. A _____ is a really big party.

 **A** What's the story? Watch the video. Number the sentences from 1 to 6. Then write the sentences in order.

_____ The group takes the subway to the parade location.

_____ Claudia talks about the music and food.

_____ Takeshi says he's hungry.

_____ The group goes to a Puerto Rican restaurant.

_____ Roberto asks a man about the parade.

__1__ Roberto says the Puerto Rican Day Parade is his favorite.

1. _____

2. _____

3. _____

4. _____

5. _____

6. _____

 B Who is speaking? Watch the video again. Circle the answers.

1. The Puerto Rican Day parade is my favorite!   (Roberto) / Sun-hee / Takeshi

2. Is it in June every year?   Sun-hee / Roberto / Claudia

3. So what do they do at the Puerto Rican Day Parade?   Claudia / Sun-hee / Takeshi

4. They play lots of cool music, and the food is delicious.   Claudia / Takeshi/ Roberto

5. Great! I'm hungry!   Takeshi / Claudia / Sun-hee

6. Where's the parade?   Roberto / Claudia / Takeshi

7. I know it's today. It's on the second Sunday in June.   Sun-hee / Roberto / Claudia

8. Let's eat!   Claudia / Roberto / Takeshi

C What do they say? Watch the video. Write the words you hear to complete the conversations.

> *Excuse me?* We're looking for the Puerto Rican Day parade.

Real English

You can say *Excuse me* to politely get a person's attention in order to ask a question.

Sun-hee: Some holidays change, like Lunar New Year.

Claudia: (1)_____*When's*_____ that?

Sun-hee: Sometimes it's in (2)_____, but I think this year it's (3)_____ February 2nd.

Roberto: Hmm . . . New Year's in (4)_____ . . . interesting.

. . . .

Takeshi: How (5)_____ does the parade last?

Roberto: Well, the parade is (6)_____ 12:00 to about 3:00, so it lasts about three hours.

Claudia: But the celebration lasts (7)_____ about 7:00 or 8:00 o'clock at night. It's really fun! Come on! The parade starts (8)_____ 15 minutes. Let's get moving.

. . . .

Roberto: Excuse me? We're looking for the Puerto Rican Day parade.

Man: Puerto Rican Day parade? That's next (9)_____. It's on the (10)_____ Sunday in (11)_____.

Roberto: Yeah, but today is . . .

Claudia: June 6th. The (12)_____ Sunday in June!

4 After You Watch

 A Study the expressions from the video in the box below. Then use the expressions to complete the conversations. Use each expression only once.

> **Useful Expressions**
> How long does it last?
> Let's get moving.
> Let's ask.
> ~~I think it's~~ . . .
> Hmm. . . interesting.

1. A: When is the party?

   B: ___I think it's___ on Friday.

2. A: This is a good TV show.

   B: Yeah. _____

   A: One hour.

3. A: My birthday's on May 3rd.

   B: _____ My birthday's on May 3rd, too!

4. A: We're late for class!

   B: OK. _____

5. A: Where's the restaurant?

   B: I'm not sure. _____

B Now, complete the conversation below. Use the expressions in A.

Raquel:	Want to go see the new Ben Affleck movie?
Mia:	__Hmm. . . interesting__. Yeah, let's go.
Raquel:	It starts in 20 minutes. We're late! _____.
Mia:	OK. _____
Raquel:	I'm not sure, but _____ two hours long.
Mia:	Where's the movie theater?
Raquel:	I don't know. _____.

Language Link: *How long*; Prepositions of time				
How long is your class?	It's **from** 7:00 **to** 9:00. It **lasts for** two hours	I was born **in**	May. 1984. the spring.	Use *in* + month, year, or season.
How long does your class last?	It **lasts until** 9:00. It's two hours **long**.	I was born **on**	May 28, 1984. the 28th of May. Sunday, the 28th.	Use *on* + specific date or day.

> The parade is from 12:00 to about 3:00.

 In the video, Roberto uses prepositions of time to talk about the Puerto Rican Day Parade. Study the box. Then complete these sentences.

1. Christmas is _____in_____ December.

2. Mary's birthday is _____ the 5th of July.

3. How _____ is the party? It's _____ 8:00 _____ 11:00.

4. Richard's party is _____ Tuesday, the 22nd.

5. She was born _____ 1988.

6. My dance class lasts _____ 3:30.

7. Is your birthday _____ the winter?

8. Chinese New Year's celebrations are often fifteen days _____!

 Complete the story summary. Use the words in the box.

sixth	three	man	music	7:00 or 8:00	~~Parade~~	second	Sunday

Roberto tells Claudia, Sun-hee, and Takeshi about the Puerto Rican Day (1)_____Parade_____. He says the parade is (2)_____ hours long. Claudia says the celebration lasts until (3)_____ at night. The group arrives at the parade location but there is no (4)_____, no food and no parade! Roberto asks a (5)_____ about the parade. The man says the parade is next (6)_____, the (7)_____ Sunday in June. The group understands the bad news – the date is June (8)_____, the first Sunday in June!

SPECIAL: RICE AND BEANS

Special Occasions

Global Viewpoints | Special Occasions

 1 Before You Watch

A Here are some words you will hear in the interviews about "Special Occasions." Write the correct word under each picture.

| fireworks | a grave | park |

1. _____   2. _____   3. _____

B Here are some more words you will hear in the interviews. Match the words with the definitions.

1. ancestors __*e*__   a. to go to see someone and spend time with them

2. blessings _____   b. to dislike someone or something very much

3. independence _____   c. done by people for a long time

4. hate _____   d. things that you feel happy or lucky to have

5. summertime _____   e. ~~relatives who lived a long time ago~~

6. take place _____   f. freedom

7. visit _____   g. to happen

8. traditional _____   h. the warm months between spring and fall

C Now, use the words in B to complete these sentences. Use each word or phrase only once.

1. We do __traditional__ dances to celebrate many holidays.

2. _____ is my favorite time of year because I love hot weather.

3. Her _____ came to Australia from Spain 100 years ago.

4. I _____ my grandmother every Sunday.

5. I don't want any vegetables! I _____ them!

6. Good health and a nice family are _____.

7. The Olympics _____ every four years.

8. The U.S. got its _____ from England in 1776.

2 While You Watch

A What special occasions do these people talk about? Watch the video and match the names with the occasions.

1. Brad __f__
2. José Luis ___
3. Julianna ___
4. Alejandra ___
5. Catherine ___
6. Jackie ___

a. New Year's Eve
b. *Carnaval*
c. a birthday
d. Mexican Independence day
e. *Chusok*
f. ~~The 4ᵗʰ of July~~

Real English

Every year my friend throws me a surprise party.

Catherine

To throw a party means to organize a party, especially in your home.

B What do these people say about the special occasions? Watch the video again and circle the words you hear.

1. Brad: I like to go to the park and watch the (fireworks) / parade.

2. José Luis: My favorite holiday / celebration is Mexican Independence Day.

3. Julianna: It takes place in February, during the summertime / wintertime.

4. Alejandra: I usually go out with my friends / boyfriend to parties to dance.

5. Catherine: Every year my friend throws me a surprise party, and I love / hate them.

6. Jackie: . . . we also visit our ancestors' graves and ask for blessings / rice cakes.

Your View on . . . *Special Occasions*

How about you? Answer the questions below.

1. What is your favorite holiday or special occasion? When is it?

   _____

2. What do you usually do on that day?

   _____

   _____

3. What do you eat and drink on that day?

   _____

   _____

9 Person to Person

City Living | Dear Mum and Dad . . .

---

1 Preview

 A In this episode, Tara sends her parents an e-mail about life in New York City.

Dear Mum and Dad, life in New York is great.

I get up early every day . . .

I always have a healthy breakfast

Tara writes an e-mail to her parents.

She tells her parents about her morning.

She writes about her eating habits.

I go to work at 4:30.

I get home at about 11:30. Sometimes I do homework . . .

She tells them about her job.

Tara explains everything she does each day . . . or does she?

B Look at the photos above. Then circle the correct answers.

1. Tara is writing to her <u>aunt and uncle / mother and father</u>.

2. She gets up <u>early / late</u>.

3. She thinks an apple is a <u>healthy / unhealthy</u> breakfast.

4. She works <u>in the morning / in the evening</u>.

5. She gets home <u>early / late</u> from her job.

A Here are some activities you will hear mentioned in the video. Match each activity with a picture.

get dressed
do homework
teach
~~check e-mail~~
get home

1. __check e-mail__   2. _____

3. _____   4. _____   5. _____

B You will hear the bolded words in the video. Circle the correct words to complete the definitions.

1. A **café** is a kind of (restaurant) / school.

2. The opposite of **early** is boring / late.

3. People who are **roommates** live / work together.

4. **Smart** means the same as intelligent / thin.

5. To "**surf the Net**" means to look at different web sites / get some exercise.

A What is Tara's schedule? Watch the video. Check (✓) the sentences that are true. Then correct the false sentences.

                                    7:30

1. ___ Tara gets up every day at ~~7:00~~.

2. ___ Sometimes she checks her e-mail after breakfast.

3. ___ She often meets Sun-hee and Claudia for lunch.

4. ___ She always studies after lunch.

5. ___ She works nights from 5:00 to 11:00.

6. ___ She is never late for work.

7. ___ She gets home from work at about 11:30.

8. ___ She usually does homework after work.

 B What is Tara saying in the video? Watch the video again and match the sentences with the pictures.

a. I always have a healthy breakfast.

b. OK, well . . . hardly ever.

c. ~~Sometimes I relax a little.~~

d. I usually just go to bed.

e. I often surf the Net.

1.   <u>c</u>   2. _____

3. _____   4. _____   5. _____

What does Tara say? Watch the video. Write the words you hear to complete these parts of Tara's e-mail message.

Real English

Dear Mum and Dad . . .

Like "mom" in American English, mum is an informal word for "mother" in British English.

Tara: I'm working at a café, too. It's not bad, but I'm really busy. I (1)_____usually_____ work nights, but I get up (2)_____ every day, about seven o'clock. Well, maybe 7:30. I get (3)_____, and then I (4)_____ have a healthy breakfast. Well, usually. After breakfast I always (5)_____ my e-mail, and I often (6)_____ the Net, but only for about an hour. Well, (7)_____ longer.

. . . .

Tara: I work nights during the week from 5:00 to 11:00, so I go to work at 4:30. I'm (8)_____ late. OK, well hardly (9)_____. Then, I get (10)_____ at about 11:30. Sometimes I do some homework, but not (11)_____. I usually just go to bed. Well, (12)_____ always to bed, but . . . ah, don't ask!

4 After You Watch

A Look at the sentences from the video in the box below. Study the expressions in red. Then match each expression with the correct definition.

> **Useful Expressions**
>
> It's not bad, but I'm really busy.
>
> Well, not always to bed, but . . . ah, don't ask.
>
> Give my love to everyone.

1. It's OK. _____

2. I don't want to talk about that. _____

3. An expression you use to end an e-mail or letter. _____

B Now, use the expressions in A to fill in the blanks. Use each expression only once.

1. A: How are you today?
   B: _____
   Things are terrible!

2. Dear Mark,
   I'm having a wonderful time on
   my vacation.
   _____
   Beth

3. A: How's your English class?
   B: _____

Language Link: Frequency adverbs

Jackie is **always** late. 100% usually often sometimes hardly ever / seldom never 0%	She isn't **usually** on time.	With *be*, frequency adverbs are after the verb.
Jackie **always** gets up at 8:00.	She doesn't **usually** get up at 7:00.	With other verbs, frequency adverbs are before the main verb.

 In the video, Tara uses frequency adverbs to talk about her schedule. Study the box. Then put the frequency adverb in the correct place in each sentence below.

I always check my e-mail and I often surf the Net...

 always
1. Nancy ‸ gets dressed before breakfast. (always)

2. Paul does his homework at night. (usually)

3. Mark and Jim are late for class. (hardly ever)

4. Julian goes to the movies on Saturday nights. (often)

5. I am at home on weekends. (seldom)

6. We go to a restaurant for lunch. (sometimes)

D Complete the story summary. Use the words in the box.

| café | ~~early~~ | e-mail | gets | has | surfs | roommates | sleep |

Tara writes an email to her parents and tells them about her life in New York. She gets up (1)___ *early* ___ every day. She gets dressed and then she (2)_____ breakfast. After breakfast, she checks her (3)_____, and she often (4)_____ the Net. She often meets her (5)_____ for lunch. After lunch, she studies or relaxes. She goes to work in a (6)_____ at 4:30. She (7)_____ home at about 11:30 and goes to (8)_____. Tara is a very busy person!

Person to Person

Global Viewpoints | Daily Activities

---

1 Before You Watch

Here are some words and phrases you will hear in the interviews about "Daily Activities." Write the correct word or phrase under each picture.

brush your teeth   drive   drums   ~~volleyball~~

1. ___volleyball___

2. _____

3. _____

4. _____

Real English

She gets up at 9:00 in the morning, washes up, and then goes to school.

Wash up has different meanings in American and British English. In American English, it means to wash yourself. In British English it means to wash the dishes after a meal.

2 While You Watch

What do these people say about daily activities? Watch the interviews and circle the answers.

1. Julianna gets up at six / (seven) A.M. every day.

2. Julianna takes the bus / drives to work.

3. Woo Sung's sister is a student at Boston / New York University.

4. Woo Sung's sister is studying / teaching psychology.

5. Hana's sister gets up at eight / nine o'clock in the morning.

6. Hana's sister has volleyball practice after school / on Saturdays.

7. Jonathan always / sometimes practices drums for two hours.

8. After work, Alejandra sometimes meets friends / goes to the gym.

Global Viewpoints | Dating

1 Before You Watch

You will hear the words below in the interviews about "Dating." Complete each sentence with the correct word.

boyfriend   pay   theater

1. My sister has a new _____. She really likes him a lot.

2. People watch movies or plays in a _____.

3. In my country, men always _____ the bill at a restaurant.

2 While You Watch

What do these people say about dating? Watch the interviews and match the names with the sentences.

1. Alejandra _____
2. Hana _____
3. José Luis _____
4. Nick _____

a. I have never had a boyfriend.
b. On the weekends, I like to go on dates.
c. On a date we both usually pay.
d. A woman almost never calls a man.

Your View on . . . *Person to Person*
How about you? Answer the questions below.

1. Who do you usually write e-mails or letters to? What do you write about?

   _____

2. Compare your schedule with Tara's. How is it different? How is it the same?

   _____

3. When is the best time for a date? On the weekend? After work? Another time?

   _____

4. What are some good places to go on a date?

   _____

10 Home Sweet Home

City Living | Welcome to New York!

1 Preview

A In this episode, we learn how Mike and Takeshi became roommates.

Mike! Welcome to New York!

Mike arrives in New York City.

My friend Takeshi needs a roommate.

Mike needs a place to live and Tara has an idea.

Is there a bed for Mike?

Tara gets some information from Takeshi.

This is the living room.

Takeshi shows them his apartment.

Uh, how much is the rent?

Mike asks an important question.

B Look at the photos above. Then answer the questions. Choose *a*, *b*, or *c*.

1. Who is new to New York City? _____

   a. Tara   b. Mike   c. Takeshi

2. Who lives in New York City? _____

   a. Tara and Mike   b. Mike and Takeshi   c. Tara and Takeshi

3. Who needs a roommate? _____

   a. Takeshi   b. Mike   c. Tara

4. Whose apartment is it? _____

   a. Tara's   b. Mike's   c. Takeshi's

5. Who wants information about the cost of the apartment? _____

   a. Tara   b. Mike   c. Takeshi

A Here are some rooms of the house you will hear about in the video. Number each room in the picture.

1. bedroom   2. kitchen   3. living room

B Here are some more words you will hear in the video. Write the correct word under each picture.

bed   chair   ~~desk~~   fridge   lamp   microwave   sofa   table

1.   desk

2. _____

3. _____

4. _____

5. _____

6. _____

7. _____

8. _____

A What's the story? Watch the video. Circle the correct words to complete the sentences.

1. Mike comes to (New York City)/ Los Angeles.

2. Takeshi needs <u>an apartment / a roommate</u>.

3. Mike and Tara go to <u>Takeshi's / Tara's</u> apartment.

4 Mike asks about <u>the rent / a job</u>.

5. Takeshi says the rent is <u>$800 / $900</u>.

6. Mike thinks the rent is <u>cheap / expensive</u>.

7. Mike wants the apartment for only one or two <u>months / years</u>.

8. Mike and Takeshi <u>are / are not</u> roommates now.

 B What are they saying? Watch the video again and match the sentences with the pictures.

So that's the story.

Welcome home!

~~Well, Tara and I were old friends.~~

There's a bed, a table, a lamp, a desk . . .

One or two months, huh?

1. Mike: <u>Well, Tara and I were old friends.</u>

2. Takeshi: _____

3. Takeshi: _____

4. Sun-hee: _____

5. Takeshi: _____

What do they say? Watch the video. Write the words you hear to complete the conversations.

> Eight hundred dollars? That's kind of *expensive for me.*

Tara: It's on the third floor. (1)___There___ are four rooms. There are two bedrooms. (2)_____ a big kitchen, and a great living room.

Mike: (3)_____ there a bed in the extra bedroom?

Tara: Is there a bed for Mike? Yes. The (4)_____ is furnished. There is a bed, a table, a lamp, a (5)_____, and, uh . . . there are two (6)_____.

Mike: Sounds terrific. Let's go!

. . . .

Takeshi: This is the (7)_____ room. There's a sofa, a (8)_____, table, TV.

Mike: Nice.

Takeshi: Over there's the (9)_____. We have a table. There are a couple of chairs, a (10)_____, a fridge. And here's the bedroom. There's a (11)_____, a table, a lamp, a desk, and there (12)_____ two chairs for you.

Mike: I'll take it!

A Look at the sentences from the video in the box below. Study the expressions in red. Then match each expression with the correct definition.

Useful Expressions

Mike: Just remember, Tara—no apartment, no job, goodbye, New York. Got it?

***

Tara: Hi, Takeshi. My friend Mike is in town.

***

Mike: Sounds terrific. Let's go.

***

Tara: See you soon!

1. a way to make a suggestion _____Let's_____

2. an expression used to say "goodbye" _____

3. a way to say that a person is visiting the city where you live _____

4. an informal way to ask, "Do you understand what I'm saying?" _____

B Now, use the expressions in A to complete the conversations. Use each expression only once.

1. A: _____go to the movies later!
   B: OK.

2. A: Let's go see "The King."
   B: Is it _____?
   A: Yeah, it's at the 4th Street Theater.

3. A: The meeting's at 3:00
      on Thursday. _____
   B: Yes.

4. A: Bye-bye!
   B: _____

Language Link: *There is / There are*		
Singular	There's a sofa in the living room. There isn't a desk in the bedroom.	Is there a desk in the bedroom? Yes, there is. / No, there isn't.
Plural	There are chairs in the kitchen. There aren't any chairs in the bedroom.	Are there two / any chairs in the kitchen? Yes, there are. / No, there aren't.

Use *there is / there are* to:
- say that something does or doesn't exist.
- say where something is or is not located.

C In the video, the characters use *there is* and *there are* to talk about Takeshi's apartment. Study the box. Then complete the conversation below.

There are *four rooms.*

Ali: (1)___There are___ six rooms in my new apartment.

Mina: Wow! That's a big apartment. (2)_____ a big living room?

Ali: No, (3)_____, but (4)_____ three bedrooms.

Mina: Is the apartment furnished?

Ali: Well, the bedroom is furnished. (5)_____ a bed, a desk, and a lamp.

Mina: (6)_____ any chairs in the bedroom?

Ali: No, (7)_____. But (8)_____ three chairs in the living room. You can use one of them!

D Complete the story summary. Use the words in the box.

> apartment   cheap   expensive   friend   town   bedroom   rooms   ~~roommates~~

We learn the story of how Takeshi and Mike became (1)_roommates_. Mike is in (2)_____ visiting his friend Tara. He has no (3)_____ and no job. Tara's (4)_____ Takeshi needs a roommate. Tara and Mike go to Takeshi's apartment. There are four (5)_____ in the apartment and there's a (6)_____ for Mike. Mike thinks $800 a month for the apartment is (7)_____. But Tara says, "For New York, that's (8)_____." Mike takes the apartment and after two years, Mike and Takeshi are still roommates!

Home Sweet Home

Global Viewpoints | Where I Live

1 Before You Watch

Here are some words you will hear in the interviews about "Where I Live." Complete each sentence with the correct word.

> parents   house   building

1. Our school is a big _____, so there are many classrooms.

2. My family lives in a big _____.

3. I live alone, but my sister lives at home with our _____.

2 While You Watch

  A Where do these people live? Watch the interviews and match the names with the information.

1. Alejandra __*e*__   a. lives in a small house with four bedrooms.

2. Jackie _____   b. lives in a house in Mexico city.

3. José Luis _____   c. lives in a house with three different rooms and a kitchen.

4. Jonathan _____   d. lives in a place with six rooms.

5. Catherine _____   e. ~~lives in a one-bedroom apartment in an old building~~.

  B Who do they live with? Watch the interviews again and circle the correct words.

1. José Luis lives with his <u>wife / parents</u>.

2. Jonathan lives with <u>six / three</u> other people.

3. Catherine lives with two <u>roommates / sisters</u>.

Real English

Right now *I live with. . .*

People usually say *right now* in a conversation to mean "now" or "at the present time."

Global Viewpoints | Student Housing

1 Before You Watch

You will hear the words below in the interviews about "Student Housing." Write the correct word under each picture.

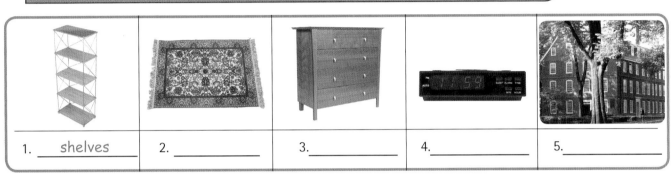

alarm clock	dorm(itory)	dresser	rug	shelves

1. shelves
2. _____
3. _____
4. _____
5. _____

2 While You Watch

What do you learn about these people? Watch the interviews and circle the correct answers.

1. Hana lives in an apartment / (a dormitory).

2. Dave has one roommate / two roommates.

3. Vanessa's room has two beds, two dressers, and two desks / closets.

4. Calum's dorm is big and new / old, and it's very noisy / quiet at night.

5. Calum's dorm room is very small / large.

Real English

That's all there's **room** for.

People sometimes use the word **room** to mean space or area.

Your View on . . . *Home Sweet Home*

How about you? Answer the questions below.

1. Do you live in an apartment, a house, or a dorm?

   _____

2. Who do you live with?

   _____

3. What rooms do you have in your home?

   _____

4. What kinds of things are there in your favorite room?

   _____

1 Preview

A In this episode, Sun-hee buys a new dress for Roberto's party.

It's a party for work.

Claudia reminds Sun-hee about Roberto's party that evening.

Wow! Look at that dress.

Sun-hee goes shopping for an outfit for the party.

$285? That's pretty expensive.

The sales clerk tells Sun-hee the price of the dress.

They're usually $125 . . . But they're on sale for $75.

Sun-hee also asks about some nice shoes.

Sun-hee buys an outfit and goes to the party, but what's wrong?

B Look at the photos above. Then circle the correct answers.

1. Claudia reminds Sun-hee about <u>a party / a dress</u>.

2. Sun-hee <u>likes / doesn't like</u> the dress.

3. Sun-hee thinks the dress is <u>expensive / inexpensive</u>.

4. The shoes are <u>more / less</u> expensive because they're on sale.

5. At the party, Sun-hee looks <u>happy/ worried</u>.

A   Here are some words you will hear in the video. Write the correct word under each picture.

~~dress~~   price   shoes   suit

$285 = two hundred (and) eighty-five dollars

1. _____dress_____   2._____   3._____   4._____

B   Here are some more words you will hear in the video. Match each word or phrase with the correct definition.

1. dark __b__   a. the opposite of casual or relaxed

2. dress up _____   b. ~~not light in color~~

3. forget _____   c. the place where a business person works

4. formal _____   d. to feel concerned or troubled about something

5. worry _____   e. to not remember

6. office _____   f. to wear nice or special clothes

C   Now, use the words in B to complete these sentences. Use each word or phrase only once.

1. Don't _____worry_____ about the rent. I have the money to pay it.

2. I work in a big _____ downtown.

3. I always _____ to check my e-mail, so I don't get your messages!

4. It's a _____ party, so wear a nice suit.

5. I don't often _____. I usually wear casual clothes.

6. Felix is wearing jeans and a _____ sweater.

3 While You Watch

 A What's the story? Watch the video. Circle the correct words to complete the sentences.

1. Claudia reminds Sun-hee about (Roberto's) / Mike's party.

2. Sun-hee thinks about what to wear to <u>work / the party</u>.

3. Sun-hee goes shopping for <u>food / clothes</u>.

4. Sun-hee asks the sales clerk about a <u>dark / light</u> dress.

5. The dress is on sale for <u>$225 / $285</u>.

6. The shoes are on sale for <u>$75 / $125</u>.

7. Sun-hee <u>dresses up / doesn't dress up</u> for the party.

8. Roberto's party is <u>formal / informal</u>.

 B What are they saying? Watch the video again. Match the sentences with the pictures.

Besides, Mike dressed up!

It's usually $285.

So, this isn't a formal party?

Wow! That's $50 off!

~~But what do I wear?~~

1. Sun-hee: <u>But what do I wear?</u>

2. Sales Clerk: _____

3. Sun-hee: _____

4. Sun-hee: _____

5. Roberto: _____

What do they say? Watch the video. Write words you hear to complete the conversations.

Real English

Excellent!

The sales clerk says Excellent! to show approval. She may mean "excellent idea" or "excellent decision."

Sun-hee:	Nice (1)_____suit_____.
Claudia:	Thanks. Hey, don't (2)_____ about Roberto's party tonight.
Sun-hee:	Oh, yeah. What kind of party is it?
Claudia:	It's a party for (3)_____. All the people from his (4)_____ are coming. See you there!

· ·

Sun-hee:	That's a beautiful (5)_____ outside.
Sales Clerk:	Oh, which one?
Sun-hee:	The (6)_____ one. How (7)_____ is it?
Sales Clerk:	It's on (8)_____. It's usually $285.

· ·

Roberto:	Hi!
Mike:	Hi, Sun-hee! You look (9)_____!
Sun-hee:	Thanks. So, this isn't a (10)_____ party?
Roberto:	Hey, don't (11)_____ about it. They're just (12)_____ from work. Besides, Mike dressed up!

4 After You Watch

A Study the expressions from the video in the box below. Then use the expressions to complete the conversations. Use each expression only once.

> **Useful Expressions**
>
> How much is it?
>
> It's on sale.
>
> That's not a bad price.
>
> ~~That's pretty expensive.~~
>
> Which one?

1. A: The watch costs $3,000.
   B: ___That's pretty expensive.___

2. A: That's a nice stereo.
   B: _____
   A: The big one.

3. A: _____
   B: It's $49.

4. A: It's only $19.99.
   B: _____

5. A: _____ It's
   usually $399, but now it's $299.
   B: Excellent! I'll take it!

B Now, number the sentences 1 to 5 to put the conversation in order.

_____ The brown one. How much is it?

_____ Are you kidding? That's pretty expensive for me!

___1___ That's a nice suit.

_____ It's on sale for $500. That's not a bad price.

_____ Which one?

Language Link: Count nouns and noncount nouns

Count nouns			Noncount nouns	
Count nouns have *a*, *an*, or a number in front of the noun. They can be singular or plural.	singular	plural	Noncount nouns don't have *a*, *an*, or a number in front of the noun. They are always singular.	money clothing art fruit jewelry
	a suit	two suits		
	a dress	three dresses		
	a store	two stores		
	a dollar	five dollars		
	an office	many offices		

C In the video, the Claudia uses a count noun to talk about the party. Study the box. Then complete the following sentences with *is* or *are*.

It's a party *for work.*

1. There _____is_____ money on the table.

2. There _____ twelve months in a year.

3. The clothing _____ on the sofa.

4. Art _____ her favorite subject.

5. Three books _____ on the desk.

6. This fruit _____ delicious.

7. Two chairs _____ in your room.

8. There _____ a grocery store near here.

D Complete the story summary. Use the words in the box.

$225	formal	dress	~~party~~	$75	shopping	wears	worry

Roberto is having a (1)__party__. The people from his office are coming. Sun-hee goes (2)_____ for something to wear. She sees a beautiful (3)_____. It's usually $285, but it's on sale for (4)_____. She also finds some shoes on sale for (5)_____. Sun-hee buys the dress and the shoes. She (6)_____ them to the party. Sun-hee looks great, but it isn't a (7)_____ party. Roberto tells Sun-hee, "Don't (8)_____ about it!" Why? Because Mike "dressed up" in a T-shirt!

Clothing

Global Viewpoints | Fashion and Colors

1 Before You Watch

A Here are some words you will hear in the interviews about "Fashion and Colors." Write the correct word under each picture.

jeans	scarf	shirt
sweatshirt	trousers	

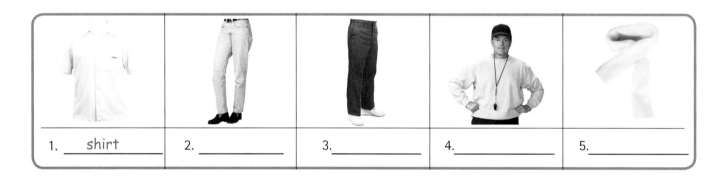

1. _shirt_   2. _____   3. _____   4. _____   5. _____

B Here are some colors mentioned in the video. Match the colors to the words.

black   purple   ~~red~~   white   yellow

 red   _____    _____   _____   _____

2 While You Watch

A What do these people say about fashion and colors? Watch the interviews and circle *True* or *False*. Correct the false sentences.

likes
1. Paula ~~doesn't like~~ to dress up.   True /(False)

2. Brad's shirt cost $11.00.   True / False

3. Dave's shoes are about five years old.   True / False

4. Catherine likes to wear casual clothes at work.   True / False

5. Dennis likes to wear black.   True / False

6. Hana likes to wear black, purple, and yellow.   True / False

7. Julianna's favorite colors are black and red.   True / False

8. Alejandra's favorite piece of clothing is a scarf.   True / False

Real English

...fashion is not everything.

Paula uses *is not everything* to mean "is not the most important thing."

Global Viewpoints | Shopping

1 Before You Watch

You will hear the words *size* and *software* in the interviews about "Shopping." Read the definitions. Then circle the correct word to complete the sentences below.

> The size tells how big or small something is.

> Software is the word for the programs that computers use.

1. This dress is the wrong <u>size / software</u>.

2. This laptop comes with a lot of <u>sizes / software</u>.

2 While You Watch

 What do these people say about shopping? Watch the interviews and circle the correct answers.

1. Catherine <u>likes /doesn't</u> like to shop.

2. Brad <u>shops / doesn't shop</u> on the Internet.

3. Alejandra <u>buys / doesn't buy</u> clothes on the Internet.

4. Hana <u>shops / doesn't shop</u> on the Internet.

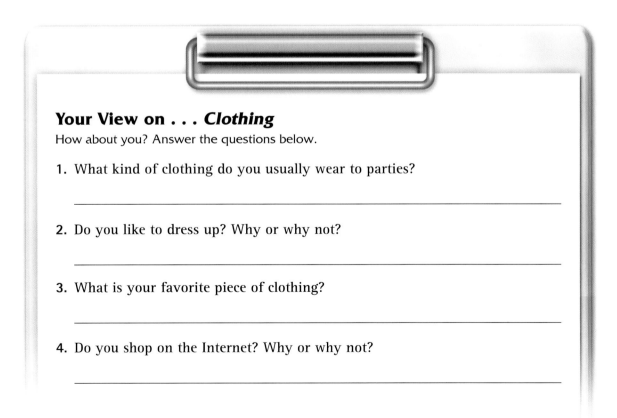

Your View on . . . *Clothing*
How about you? Answer the questions below.

1. What kind of clothing do you usually wear to parties?

   _____

2. Do you like to dress up? Why or why not?

   _____

3. What is your favorite piece of clothing?

   _____

4. Do you shop on the Internet? Why or why not?

   _____

Jobs and Ambitions

City Living | I can get this job!

1 Preview

 A In this episode, Roberto helps Mike prepare for a job interview.

... I really want this job.

Mike tells Roberto about an important job interview.

Trust me. I know this.

Roberto has some time and offers to help Mike prepare.

What are you like?

Roberto asks Mike a few interview questions.

I know I can get this job!

Mike gets excited about the interview.

What kind of job interview is this?

Then Roberto asks one more important question.

B Look at the photos above and circle *True* or *False*. Then correct the false sentences.

1. Mike has an interview for a job.   True / False

2. Roberto really wants the job.   True / False

3. Roberto helps Mike practice for the interview.   True / False

4. In the end, Mike feels ready for the interview.   True / False

5. Roberto knows what job Mike is interviewing for.   True / False

Here are some adjectives you will hear in the video. Use the words to complete the sentences.

creative   funny   ~~hardworking~~
outgoing   shy

1. She's <u>hardworking</u>. 2. He's _____. 3. She's _____. 4. He's _____. 5. She's _____.

 Here are some additional words you will hear in the video. Use the words to complete the sentences.

1. They <u>swim</u> in the city pool on Saturdays.

appointment   flexible   full-time
~~swim~~   part-time

2. Amy has a _____ job. She works 15 hours a week.

3. Laura has a doctor's _____ at 9:00 tomorrow morning.

4. Carl can easily change his schedule. He's very _____.

5. It's a _____ job. I have to work 40 hours a week.

C Here are some more words you will hear in the video. Write the correct word under each picture.

bathing suit   lifeguard   ~~receptionist~~   résumé   waiter

1. <u>receptionist</u> 2. _____ 3. _____ 4. _____ 5. _____

A What's the story? Watch the video. Number the sentences from 1 to 6 to put them in order. Then write the sentences in order.

_____ Roberto looks at Mike's résumé.

__1__ Mike is worried about the job interview.

_____ Mike says he can't swim but he looks good in a bathing suit.

_____ Roberto says he can help Mike prepare for the interview.

_____ Mike practices answering interview questions.

_____ Roberto asks Mike what job the interview is for.

1. _____

2. _____

3. _____

4. _____

5. _____

6. _____

B What does Mike say to Roberto? Watch the video and circle *a* or *b*.

1. **Roberto:** What time is the interview?

   (a.) It's today at three o'clock.　　　　b. It's tomorrow at three o'clock.

2. **Roberto:** So, are you looking for a full-time or a part-time job?

   a. Full-time.　　　　b. Full-time or part-time.

3. **Roberto:** What do you do now?

   a. I have two jobs right now.　　　　b. Well, I don't have a job right now.

4. **Roberto:** What languages do you speak?

   a. I speak Spanish . . .　　　　b. I can write Spanish very well.

5. **Roberto:** What else can you do?

   a. I can use a Mac.　　　　b. I can use PCs and Macs.

6. **Roberto:** Can you swim?

   a. Yes, I can.　　　　b. No, I can't.

What do they say? Watch the video. Write the words you hear to complete the conversations.

Real English

Now go get 'em!

The informal expression go get 'em means "good luck" or "do your best" ('em = them).

Roberto:	I have some time before my (1) _appointment_ . I can help you.
Mike:	What are you doing?
Roberto:	I'm (2)_____ you. I'm a businessman. Trust me. I know this. Sit down.
	Welcome, Mr. Johnson. Do you have your (3)_____?
Mike:	Yes. Here you are, Mr. Chavez.

• •

Roberto:	Let's see. An actor, a waiter, a painter, a singer, a (4)_____. Wow, that's a lot of jobs. So, are you looking for a (5)_____ or a part-time job?
Mike:	Full-time or part-time. I'm (6)_____.
Roberto:	I see. What do you (7)_____ now?
Mike:	Well, I don't have a job right now.

• •

Roberto:	Hey, by the way, what kind of job interview is this?
Mike:	It's a (8)_____ for a lifeguard down at the city (9)_____.
Roberto:	A lifeguard? (10)_____ you (11)_____?
Mike:	No, I (12)_____. But I look good in a bathing suit!

4 After You Watch

A Look at the conversations from the video in the box below. Study the expressions in red. Then circle the correct definition for each below.

Useful Expressions

1. Roberto: Do you have your résumé?
   Mike: Yes. Here you are, Mr. Chavez.

2. Mike: How am I doing?
   Roberto: You're doing fine.

3. Roberto: So, are you looking for a full-time or a part-time job?
   Mike: Full-time or part-time. I'm flexible.
   Roberto: I see.

4. Roberto: What do you do now?
   Mike: Well, I don't have a job right now.

1. a. something people say when they receive something
    b. something people say when they give something

2. a. a way to ask how someone is
    b. a way to ask if you are doing things correctly

3. a. an expression that means "I understand"
    b. an expression that means "I can see you"

4. a. a way to ask what someone's job is
    b. a way to greet someone

B Now, use the expressions in A to complete the conversations.

1. A: _____
   B: Don't worry! You're doing fine!

2. A: _____
   B: I'm a lifeguard.

3. A: Can I use your cell phone?
   B: Yes. _____

4. A: So you push this button to start. Got it?
   B: Yes, _____

Language Link: Talking about abilities—*can* and *can't*			

I
You
He/She can swim.
We
They
	I
	You
	He/She can't swim.
	We
	They
		I
		you
		Can he/she swim?
		we
		they
			Yes, I can.
			No, you
			     he/she can't.
			     we
			     they

 C In the video, Mike uses *can* to talk about his abilities. Study the box. Then use *can* or *can't* to complete the following conversation.

> *I can use PCs and Macs.*

Carla: You look worried.

Kevin: I am. I (1)__can't__ do my Spanish homework.

Carla: Don't worry. I (2)_____ help you.

Kevin: (3)_____ you speak Spanish very well?

Carla: No, I (4)_____. But I (5)_____ read and write it well.

Kevin: Good. (6)_____ you read this for me?

Carla: Sorry, I (7)_____ do it now, I have class.

Kevin: That's OK. We (8)_____ do it later.

D Complete the story summary. Use the words in the box.

> creative   bathing suit   excited   ~~interview~~   lifeguard   résumé   can   swim

    Mike has an important job (1)_interview_ today. Roberto is helping him prepare for it. Roberto looks at Mike's (2)_____ and asks him interview questions. Mike says he's smart and (3)_____ and he (4)_____ use PCs and Macs. He gets really (5)_____ about the job. When Roberto finds out the job is for a (6)_____, he asks, "Can you (7)_____?" Mike says he can't swim, but he looks good in a (8)_____!

Jobs and Ambitions

Global Viewpoints | My Job

Here are some words you will hear in the interviews about "My Job." Use the words to complete the sentences.

| bank | lawyer | fix | mall | ~~organized~~ | quick-thinking |

1. My sister is very _organized_ —even her desk is neat.

2. We go shopping at the _____ every weekend.

3. The thief called his _____ from the police station.

4. I need some money. Is there a _____ near here?

5. _____ people get ideas fast.

6. Can you _____ this broken chair?

2 While You Watch

A What do these people do? Watch the interviews. Match the names with the correct information.

1. Brad _f_   a. is a lawyer.

2. Vanessa ____   b. is an international student advisor.

3. Kumiko ____   c. works in a bank and at a mall.

4. Julianna ____   d. is a teacher.

5. Catherine ____ e. is a financial manager.

6. Alejandra ____ f. ~~is a student and a technician.~~

> **Real English**
>
> *I like being a lawyer because I **get to** help people.*
>
> If you **get to** do something, you have an opportunity to do it.

B What do these people say about their jobs? Watch the video again and circle the words you hear.

1. Brad: I help students and teachers (fix) / use their computers.

2. Vanessa: I have a job at the bank, and a job at <u>the mall / a school</u> . . .

3. Kumiko: I like my job because it's so <u>interesting / much fun</u>.

4. Julianna: I like my job because I like to work with <u>numbers / customers</u>.

5. Catherine: I also like being a lawyer because you get to <u>learn / talk</u> a lot . . .

6. Alejandra: I love my job because I meet a lot of <u>interesting / nice</u> people.

Global Viewpoints | People at Work

1 Before You Watch

You will hear the words *friendly* and *serious* in the interviews about "People at Work." Read the definitions. Then circle the correct word to complete the sentences.

> **Friendly** people are pleasant and helpful.

> **Serious** people often think a lot and don't laugh much.

1. He works hard and never smiles. He is very <u>friendly / serious</u>.

2. I like working here. Everyone is nice and very <u>friendly / serious</u>.

2 While You Watch

 Now, watch the interviews and circle *True* or *False*. Correct the false sentences.

1. The people in Brad's office are hardworking and friendly.   (True) / False

2. Vanessa's co-workers are funny and outgoing.   True / False

3. Kumiko's co-teachers are hardworking and always serious.   True / False

4. The people in Alejandra's office are hardworking and serious.   True / False

Your View on . . . *Jobs and Ambitions*
How about you? Answer the questions below.

1. What good personal qualities or skills do you have?

   _____

2. What's your dream job? What personal qualities or skills do you need to do it?

   _____

3. What three adjectives describe you best?

   _____

4. What are the people you study or work with like?

   _____

accounting information systems (4)
actor (1)
actress (1)
afternoon (7)
alarm clock (10)
American (2)
American history (4)
ancestors (8)
anthropology (4)
a piece of toast (5)
appointment (12)
April (8)
a turkey sandwich (5)
arrive (at work) (7)
at night (7)
at noon (7)
August (8)
aunt (6)

bacon (5)
bank (12)
bathing suit (12)
beans (5)
beautiful (2)
bed (10)
bedroom (10)
Beijing (2)
big (2)
birthday (3)
black (11)
blessings (8)
book (7)
boring (2)
boyfriend (9)
Brasilia (2)
Brazil (2)
Brazilian (2)
brother (6)
building (10)
business (4)
business law (4)
busy (4)

café (9)
camera store (3)
capital (city) (2)
CD player (3)
celebration (8)
cereal (5)
chair (10)
cheap (2)
check e-mail (9)
chicken (5)
China (2)
Chinese (2)

Chinese literature (4)
chocolate (3)
city (2)
class (7)
classmate (4)
coffee (5)
come back (home) (7)
communications (4)
computer (3)
computer engineer (1)
cooking (v) (4)
corn (5)
country (2)
cousin (6)
creative (12)
crowded (2)
currently (6)
cute (4, 6)

dad (father)
dance (v) (4)
dark (11)
date (event) (4)
daughter (6)
December (8)
delicious (8)
desk (10)
difficult (2)
digital camera (3)
dinner (7)
do homework (9)
doorbell (1)
dorm(itory) (10)
dress (n) (11)
dress up (11)
dresser (10)
DVD player (3)

early (9)
earrings (3)
easy (2)
economics (4)
education (4)
eggs (5)
electronics (store) (3)
empty (2)
exercise (v) (4)
expensive (2)

family (7)
famous (1)
fantastic (3)
father (dad) (6)
favorite (1)
February (8)

fiancé (6)
fireworks (8)
first name (1)
fish (n) (5)
fix (12)
flexible (12)
food (1)
forget (11)
formal (11)
French (4)
fridge (10)
friendly (12)
from (2)
fruit (5)
full-time (12)
fun (2)
funny (12)

get dressed (9)
get home (9)
get up (7)
gift (3)
go to bed (7)
go to the movies (7)
go to school (7)
go to sleep (7)
grave (n) (8)
great (1)
guitar (3)

hardworking (12)
hate (8)
have a yoga class (7)
health and wellness (4)
heavy (3)
house (10)
hungry (8)
husband (6)

ice cream (5)
independence (8)
inexpensive (3)
interesting (2)
in the afternoon (7)
in the morning (7)

January (8)
jeans (11)
July (8)
June (8)

karaoke (machine) (3)
kitchen (10)
Korea (2)
Korean (2)

lamp (10)
laptop (computer) (3)
last name (1)
lawyer (12)
leave for work (7)
lifeguard (12)
lightweight (3)
living room (10)

mall (12)
March (8)
married (6)
May (8)
meet (a person) (7)
Mexican (2)
Mexico (2)
Mexico City (2)
microwave (10)
milk (5)
mix (n) (2)
modern (2)
morning (7)
mother (mom) (6)
movies (7)
movie star (1)
MP3 player (3)
mushrooms (5)

name (first / last) (1)
nationality (2)
Net (the) (9)
nephew (6)
new (3)
news reporter (1)
New Year's Day (8)
nickname (1)
niece (6)
night (7)
noisy (2)
noon (7)
November (8)
number (1)

October (8)
office (11)
old (2)
older (6)
orange juice (5)
organized (12)
outgoing (12)

painter (4)
painting (n) (4)
parade (8)
parents (10)
park (n) (8)

part-time (12)
party (7)
pasta (5)
pay (v) (9)
phone number (1)
piano (7)
picture (4)
player (soccer) (1)
pool (swimming) (12)
practice piano (7)
prepare dinner (7)
pretty (2)
price (11)
Puerto Rican (8)
purple (11)

quick-thinking (12)
quiet (2)

radio (3)
receptionist (12)
red (11)
relax (7)
résumé (12)
rice (5)
ring (3)
room (10)
roommates (9)
rug (10)

salad (5)
sausage (5)
scarf (11)
sculpting (4)
sculptor (4)
semester (4)
September (8)
Seoul (2)
serious (12)
shelves (10)
shirt (11)
shoes (11)
shopping (v) (4)
shower (7)
shy (12)
singer (1)
single parent (6)
sister (6)
size (11)
sleeping (v) (4)
small (2)
smart (6, 9, 12)
smell (n) (5)
soccer player (1)
sociology (4)
sofa (10)

software (11)
son (6)
speakers (audio) (3)
spend time with (family) (7)
spelled (1)
steak (5)
stereo (system) (3)
student (1)
studying (v)(4)
suit (11)
summertime (8)
sunglasses (1)
surf the Net (9)
sweatshirt (11)
swim (12)
(swimming) pool (12)

table (10)
taking (a class) (v) (4)
take place (8)
take a shower (7)
talking (v) (4)
taste (n) (5)
tea (5)
teach (9)
terrible (3)
texture (5)
theater (9)
toast (n)(5)
tomatoes (5)
traditional (8)
trousers (11)
T-shirt (3)
TV (television) (3)

ugly (2)
uncle (6)
United States (the U.S.) (2)

visit (v) (8)
waiter (12)
waiting (4)
wake up / get up (7)
Washington DC (2)
watching (v) (4)
white (11)
wife (6)
work (7)
work out at the gym (7)
worry (11)
get up (7)
yellow (11)
yoga (7)
yogurt (5)
younger (6)

Unit 1: City Living

Please, call me Dave.

Mike:	Tom Cruise. Harrison Ford. Actors have great names. I'm an actor, and my name's Mike Johnson.
Tara:	What's a great name?
Mike:	I don't know. But I want a great name.
Takeshi:	OK, Mr. Movie Star. What's your name?
Mike:	*(to camera)* They call me Bond. James Bond. Hi, I'm Keanu Reeves, nice to meet you.
Tara:	. . . and my name's Jennifer Lopez!
Takeshi:	Huh?
Tara:	But you can call me J-Lo.
Mike:	OK. J-Lo. Nice to meet you. You're my favorite actress and singer. So, uh . . . what's your phone number?
Tara:	Excuse me? My phone number? Uh-uh!
Claudia:	Mike! Takeshi! Tara!
Tara:	*(Mike does a martial arts move)* Hmm. . . are you Jim Carrey?
Mike:	No. I'm Jackie Chan.
Tara:	Oh no, you're not.
Claudia:	Thanks, Mrs. Hamilton.
Mrs. Hamilton:	You're welcome, Claudia.
Claudia:	Bye.
Mrs. Hamilton:	Bye.
Tara:	*(to camera)* Good afternoon everyone. This is news reporter Katie Couric, and here we have the famous soccer player, David Beckham. Hi David.
Mike:	Hi Katie. But, please, call me Dave.
Claudia:	And call me Julia Roberts.
Mike and Tara:	Claudia!
Claudia:	Come on you three. We're late for the movie!
Mike:	After you, J-Lo?
Tara:	After you, Dave.
Mike:	OK.
Takeshi:	Cut!

Unit 1: Global Viewpoints

Introductions

Woo Sung:	Hi, my name is Woo Sung Chung.
Dayanne:	Hi, my name is Dayanne Leal. My nickname is Day. D-A-Y.

Jonathan:	Hi, I'm Jonathan Najman. My nickname is Johnny.
Agnes:	Hi. I am Agnes Tounkara. My first name, Agnes, is spelled A-G-N-E-S. My last name is spelled T-O-U-N-K-A-R-A.
Brad:	My name is Brad Fotsch. My first name, Brad, is spelled B-R-A-D. My last name Fotsch, is spelled F-O-T-S-C-H.
Calum:	Hi. My name is Calum Docherty. I'm from Glasgow in Scotland. I'm 18 years old and I'm a student at Harvard University.
Jonathan:	I'm from Guatemala City, Guatemala, and I'm a computer engineer.
Hana:	Hi, my name is Hana Lee. I'm 20 years old. I'm a student at Boston College and I'm from Douglaston, New York.

People We Like

Dayanne:	My favorite actor is Antonio Banderas.
Woo Sung:	My favorite actress is Julia Roberts.
Kevin:	My favorite actress is Angelina Jolie because I think she is the most beautiful woman in the world.

Unit 2: City Living

Where is it?

Tara:	*(rings bell)* OK. Game time! Let's play "Where is it?" This is my favorite game. Ready?
All:	Yes. Yeah. OK.
Claudia:	OK. But it is so crowded. And this game is so boring!
Takeshi:	No it isn't. It's interesting . . .
Mike:	And cheap!
Tara:	Here we go! What country is it? It's big. It's really interesting. Beijing is a famous city there.
Roberto:	That's easy. China!
Tara:	Correct! Your turn!
Roberto:	OK. What city is it? It's in South America. It's a beautiful city, and my favorite person is from there. *(to Claudia)* Shh!
Tara:	Who's your favorite person, Roberto?
Mike:	Ooh! *(to Claudia)* Where are you from? Are you from São Paulo? Brasilia?
Sun-hee:	I know. You're from Rio!
Claudia:	Yes! I'm from Rio de Janeiro!
Sun-hee:	*(to Roberto)* It's Rio!
Roberto:	*(rings bell)* You are correct!

Sun-hee:	Yay! My turn! What city is it? It's expensive . . . and cheap. It's noisy . . . and quiet. It's modern . . . but some places are old.
All:	Huh? What?
Sun-hee:	OK. It's in the U.S. It's crowded. People from all over the world live there—Mexicans, Koreans, Brazilians, Japanese . . .
Claudia:	I know. It's right here. It's New York City!
Sun-hee:	You're correct!
Claudia:	Yay! My turn!
Mike:	Uh-uh! Wait a minute! *(imitating Claudia)* "This game is so boring!"
Claudia:	No, it's not. It's exciting! It's fun! Come on, Mike! Come on . . . .

Unit 2: Global Viewpoints

Where I'm From

Kumiko:	I'm from Tokyo, Japan. Tokyo is a big city. There are lots of people. And it's very noisy and crowded.
Jonathan:	I'm from the country of Guatemala and I live in the capital city of Guatemala. Guatemala City is noisy.
Paula:	I am Brazilian. I'm from Belo Horizonte.
Dayanne:	I am from a city called São Paulo. São Paulo is a very big city.
Dennis:	I was born in Manila, Philippines. Manila is a crowded city. But it's. . . it's very pretty because it has the old and the new in one big place.
Calvin:	My city in Korea is Ulsan.
Woo Sung:	I'm from Paramus, New Jersey. Paramus is a big, beautiful, modern city.
Agnes:	I live in Dakar, which is the capital of Senegal. Dakar is a very interesting city because it's a mix of old and new.

Favorite Cities

Brad:	My favorite city in the world is Barcelona, Spain.
Vanessa:	Boston is my favorite city.
Woo Sung:	I like Boston because it is not too big, but it is beautiful.
José Luis:	Mexico City is a big, noisy but beautiful city.
Calum:	My favorite city is Singapore.
Kumiko:	My favorite city is Sydney, Australia. Sydney is such a beautiful city and Australian people are very kind.
Jonathan:	My favorite city in the whole world is New York.

Unit 3: City Living

A Cool Gift

Sun-hee:	Wow. Here's a cool gift for Tara's birthday.
Mike:	Gee, that's expensive.
Sun-hee:	Oh, come on, Mike.
Mike:	OK. But only for Tara's gift.
Salesman:	Hi. May I help you?
Mike:	Yes. Is this a good DVD player?
Salesman:	Oh yes. It's a very nice DVD player and it's inexpensive. It's only a hundred and twenty-nine dollars.
Mike:	One hundred and twenty-nine dollars? That's inexpensive?
Sun-hee:	But it's really nice Mike, and it's a really cool gift. *(to salesman)* We'll take it!
Mike:	I don't know . . . *(sees something and walks off)* Ooh . . .
Salesman:	This DVD player really is a great gift. It's inexpensive and it's lightweight.
Sun-hee:	Yeah, it is. Oh. And those TVs are great too.
Salesman:	Oh, these TVs are great. And this one has an excellent rating. It's five stars. . .
Mike:	*(adjusting dials on stereo)* Wow. A radio . . . a CD player . . . an MP3 player . . . and karaoke? This is so cool!
Sun-hee:	Five stars, huh? I like it a lot. Hmm. A new TV . . . maybe . . .
Mike:	Sun-hee! These speakers are fantastic! My old speakers are terrible, and these are really great! And this stereo is really cheap!
Salesman:	Excuse me! Your new digital camera!
Mike:	Oh! Thank you so much!
Salesman:	My pleasure!
Sun-hee:	*(to Mike)* Only Tara's gift, huh?
Mike:	Ha!

Unit 3: Global Viewpoints

Personal Items

Dennis:	In my room, I have a very small, inexpensive compact disc player.
Agnes:	In my room at home I have a small CD player, a large-screen TV, and a laptop.
Woo Sung:	In my room there is a heavy computer, an inexpensive CD player, and a modern stereo.
Agnes:	My favorite item is my CD player, because I can listen to music and I love music.
Brad:	I have a guitar. It is my favorite item, and my mother gave it to me.

Dayanne:	This is my favorite T-shirt. I like it because the cause is very important to me.
Alejandra:	This is my favorite ring. I love it because of its color.
Hana:	My favorite item is my laptop because I have a lot of pictures inside it and I can go on the Internet. It's very cool.

Favorite Gifts

Catherine:	I like big earrings. These earrings are from my boyfriend and I like them a lot.
Agnes:	My favorite gift is a camera because I love to take pictures.
Alejandra:	My favorite gift is a big box of chocolate because I love chocolate.

Unit 4: City Living

What are you doing—now?

Tara:	*(phone rings)* Hello?
Claudia:	Hi Tara. It's me. I'm calling you on my new cell phone! Look. Here I am! *(takes picture with cell phone)*
Tara:	Cool!
Claudia:	What are you doing?
Tara:	I'm studying. I'm taking an art history class this semester and I'm not doing so well.
Claudia:	What are you studying?
Tara:	Look. *(takes picture with cell phone)*
Claudia:	Hey! That's the Mona Lisa. I love that painting.
Tara:	Me too. So, what are you doing?
Claudia:	Talking on the phone. I'm shopping right now. And I have a date with Roberto for dinner at his house later. He's taking an Italian cooking class. I just love Italian food...
Tara:	That's cool. Well, have fun.
Claudia:	OK. I'll call you later. Bye. *(to street)* Taxi!
Tara:	*(phone rings)* Hello?
Claudia:	Hi Tara. It's Claudia. What are you doing? Are you studying?
Tara:	No, I'm not studying. I'm exercising now.
Claudia:	I'm waiting for Roberto. Hey! Here he is now! *(takes picture with cell phone)*
Sun-hee:	*(phone rings)* Hello?
Claudia:	Sun-hee?
Sun-hee:	Yeah.
Claudia:	Hi. It's Claudia.
Sun-hee:	Oh, hi Claudia.
Claudia:	What are you doing?
Sun-hee:	Oh, just watching TV.

Claudia:	Oh, where's Tara?
Sun-hee:	Tara? *(Tara mines sleeping)* Uh... she's sleeping.
Claudia:	Really? Gee, that's too bad.
Sun-hee:	Why? What are you up to?
Claudia:	Roberto and I are out dancing. We're at the Cat Club with Roberto's classmate Miguel. He's pretty cute—see? *(takes picture with cell phone)*
Sun-hee:	*(whispers to Tara)* Roberto's friend.
Claudia:	Too bad you two are busy. Got to go! Bye!
Sun-hee:	*(to Tara)* They're dancing. *(both wait a moment and run out door)*

Unit 4: Global Viewpoints

At School

Jackie:	I study education and English. I'm taking four classes and they are French 101, American History, Chinese Literature, and Education.
Woo Sung:	I am a junior in college and I am studying economics and business. I am taking four courses and they are anthropology, economics, sociology, and history. I'm doing well in economics and sociology.
Dave:	I study art. I'm taking five classes. I'm not doing very well in painting or in sculpting because I'm just not a very good painter or sculptor.
Brad:	I'm a senior in college and I'm studying music production and engineering. I'm taking seven classes in college right now, including art history, music history, health and wellness, and music recording.
Calvin:	I'm taking business law and accounting information systems.
Hana:	I am taking five classes. I'm studying communications and music. I'm doing well in my music classes.
Agnes:	I am a Ph.D. student and I'm studying economics. I'm not taking classes. I'm writing my final paper.

Unit 5: City Living

Takeshi's Food Video

Takeshi:	So you push here, OK?
Mike:	No problem!
Takeshi:	OK, Mike...
Mike:	I know... I know... I understand, Takeshi!
Takeshi:	Well, OK. Here's the videotape. *(knock at door)*
Mike:	Hi, Tara. Hi, Claudia.
Tara:	Hi, guys!
Takeshi:	Hi, you two.
Claudia:	Hey.

Tara:	Hi. So, what are we doing today?
Takeshi:	We're making a video about food and eating habits for my film class.
Claudia:	Great! I love food!
Tara:	Me too!
Takeshi:	Now Mike, is the camera working?
Mike:	Yep! Everything's set. The light's on.
Takeshi:	Sounds good. Let's start. *(to Claudia)* So tell me, what do you have for breakfast?
Claudia:	For breakfast I have fruit, yogurt, and orange juice.
Takeshi:	Hmm, that's pretty healthy. Do you have any coffee or tea?
Claudia:	Nope. I don't drink coffee. I don't like the caffeine—and no tea either. I really don't like the taste.
Takeshi:	Hmm, I see. Now, how about you, Tara? Do you have a healthy breakfast too?
Claudia:	Ha! She is not healthy! She has a really big English breakfast every day.
Tara:	Not every day!
Takeshi:	Well, what's an English breakfast?
Tara:	Well, it has eggs, bacon, sausage, tomatoes, mushrooms, beans, toast . . .
Takeshi:	Wow! That is a big breakfast. How about lunch and dinner?
Tara:	For lunch I usually have a salad. And I work at a restaurant, so I have dinner there . . . perhaps chicken or steak.
Takeshi:	That sounds good. How about you, Claudia? Do you like steak?
Claudia:	No, I don't eat steak. I'm a vegetarian.
Takeshi:	Wow, you are healthy, aren't you!
Tara:	*(to Claudia)* Yeah right. What about all that junk food you eat?
Claudia:	I don't eat junk food.
Tara:	Yes you do! You eat chips, chocolate, ice cream . . .
Claudia:	Well, I get hungry . . .
Takeshi:	*(to girls)* OK . . . OK. Don't worry. We're finished. That was great! *(to Mike)* How's the recording going?
Mike:	Good!
Takeshi:	Uh . . . Mike? What's that? *(indicates video tape on chair)*
Mike:	What? That? *(holding up video tape)* It's a videotape. Cut?

Unit 5: Global Viewpoints

Meals

Kumiko:	For breakfast I have a piece of toast and a cup of coffee.
Alejandra:	For breakfast I usually have coffee with milk, fruit, yogurt, and cereal.
Woo Sung:	I usually don't have breakfast.
Jonathan:	For lunch I make a turkey sandwich.

Agnes:	I have rice with fish or meat.
Woo Sung:	For lunch I eat a sandwich and have some fruit. For dinner I eat some meat with corn or rice.
Agnes:	Usually for dinner I eat pasta with vegetables. I love pasta!
Calvin:	I usually do not eat dinner.

Likes and Dislikes

Dennis:	I love to eat and I love to cook.
Denise:	My son Ricardo loves hamburgers.
Alejandra:	I don't eat meat because I don't like it.
Kumiko:	I don't like beans. I don't like the taste and the texture.
Kevin:	My favorite food is Japanese sushi.
Jonathan:	My favorite food is *quesadilla de mole*. It is a Mexican dish. *Quesadilla de mole* is a tortilla with chicken and cheese and brown sauce.
Jackie:	I don't really have a favorite food because I like mostly everything.
Catherine:	My favorite food right now is very, very simple. I like a bowl of white rice and *kimchi*, which is hot, spicy Korean cabbage. That's all I need.

Unit 6: City Living

Roberto's Family Picture

Claudia:	Hey Roberto! How's it going?
Roberto:	Well, life's definitely not boring. My little niece Rita is visiting from Los Angeles. She's sleeping right now, but wow! Busy, busy, busy!
Claudia:	How nice. How old is she?
Roberto:	She's twelve. She's my sister Louisa's daughter.
Claudia:	*(sees drawing)* Hey. What's that?
Roberto:	It's Rita's picture of our family.
Claudia:	Oh, it's beautiful. And wow! How many people are there in your family?
Roberto:	A lot! I have a really big family.
Claudia:	Yeah, you do . . . who's that?
Roberto:	This is my mother, Raquel, and this is my father, Silvio. And this is my sister Louisa, Rita's mom, and her husband Rico.
Claudia:	OK . . . and these two? What are their names?
Roberto:	That's Marco, my older brother, and this is Tomas, his son. He's a single parent.
Claudia:	And . . . who are they?
Roberto:	They're my cousins, Emilio and Olivia.
Claudia:	They look pretty cool. How old are they?
Roberto:	Let's see, Emilio is twenty-three and Olivia is twenty-six. And these people . . . are some of my aunts and uncles. My mom has three brothers. And my father has two sisters an d a brother. And then there are their wives and husbands . . .

Rita:	(entering from bedroom) Hi.
Claudia:	Hi! You must be Rita! Nice to meet you. I'm Claudia.
Rita:	Hi, Claudia. Nice to meet you too.
Claudia:	This is a beautiful drawing, Rita. Which one is you?
Rita:	This is me.
Claudia:	Say . . . where's Roberto? Is this him?
Rita:	No. That's Grampa Martinez.
Claudia:	Grampa? How old is he?
Rita:	I don't know. But he's really old—just like Uncle Roberto.

Unit 6: Global Viewpoints

My Family

Hana:	My mom's name is Helen and my dad's name is James. This is my mom, this is my dad, and this is me.
Yelena:	This is a picture of my family. This is my mother, my nephew, my brother and me.
Alejandra:	I have a brother Ivan, who is older, and a sister Anna, who is younger.
José Luis:	I have three brothers and two sisters.
Agnes:	I have a very big family in Senegal. I have twelve uncles and aunts and many, many cousins.
Brad:	I have a very small family. I have no brothers or sisters.

All about Me

Nick:	I'm twenty-three years old and I'm single.
Agnes:	I am thirty-one years old and I'm married. My husband's name is Gibrael. We have a son. His name is Kareem and he is two years old.
Denise:	I have a son. His name is Ricardo and he's ten years old.
Alejandra:	I am a single woman and I have no children.
Natalie:	I am a single mother. My daughter is two years old. Her name is Leilanni and her birthday is April sixteenth.
Yelena:	I am married. I have a husband. No kids yet . . .
Kumiko:	This is my husband. His name is Paul Lieber.
Kevin:	I am not married. . .which means I am currently single.
Catherine:	My fiancé's name is Paul Ham. I like him a lot because he is very, very smart, and he's pretty cute.

Unit 7: City Living

Mike's "Busy" Day

Takeshi:	Hey Mike.
Mike:	Shh! I'm watching my favorite show.
Takeshi:	Mike, you really need to get a job.
Mike:	A job? I'm too busy for a job.
Takeshi:	Busy? You don't work, you don't go to school. What do you do all day?
Mike:	A lot of things.
Takeshi:	Like what?
Mike:	Well, in the morning I work out at the gym.
Takeshi:	Yeah.
Mike:	And then in the afternoon I relax.
Takeshi:	But Mike, that's not work. . .
Mike:	Well, OK. What day is it today?
Takeshi:	It's Tuesday.
Mike:	OK. Well, I'm relaxing today, because I have a busy schedule tomorrow.
Takeshi:	Oh really?
Mike:	Yeah. At nine o'clock I have my yoga class. And then at noon I have lunch . . . hey, don't laugh, it's an important meal. (voice over) And then at 4:45 I have my film class.
Takeshi:	Mike, that's not a class. You go to the movies on Wednesday afternoons.
Mike:	Go to the movies. . . go to film class. . . same thing. Anyway, on Wednesday nights, I spend time with Maria.
Takeshi:	Maria? Who's Maria?
Mike:	She's a friend.
Takeshi:	What kind of friend?
Mike:	You know. A "friend" friend.
Takeshi:	Like a girlfriend? Where does she live?
Mike:	She lives here in New York.
Takeshi:	What does she do?
Mike:	She's an actress. Yeah. She's really great. She's an actress. She's a singer. She works out. She's beautiful. She's really successful.
Takeshi:	Wow. She sounds terrific. When can I meet her?
Mike:	Actually . . . right now. (turns on TV) Here she is. She's on Wednesdays at 7:30 at night, but on Tuesdays she's on channel four in the afternoon.
Takeshi:	Your girlfriend is on television?
Mike:	Well, she's not really my girlfriend . . . but I watch her all the time on TV. Isn't she beautiful?

Unit 7: Global Viewpoints

Times and Schedules

José Luis:	I wake up early, I take a shower and after breakfast I go to work.
Hana:	I get up at seven o'clock in the morning every day. And then I go to practice piano.
Reda:	I don't get up early in the morning. I get up late in the morning.

Dave:	I go to class from about ten to about five. Then I come back and I eat dinner and I do some work.
Paula:	I like to wake up at nine o'clock and by the time I go to bed it's really late, about midnight.
Woo Sung:	I wake up at ten a.m. I go to sleep at two a.m. That's college life!
Catherine:	Around 7:30 I leave for work and I arrive at work around 8:30 and I work until four o'clock. And I come back from work and I prepare dinner and I eat dinner with my friends and then we watch some TV, I read and that's it for the night.

Weekend Activities

José Luis:	On the weekend I go to parties with my friends.
Kumiko:	My husband and I often go to restaurants.
Brad:	On the weekends I like to relax and sleep late. At night I go to dinner and a movie with my girlfriend Lara. My girlfriend Lara is a student. On weekends she goes shopping, works out at the gym, and reads lots of books.

Unit 8: City Living

I love parades!

Claudia:	I love parades!
Roberto:	Me too! The Puerto Rican Day Parade is my favorite.
Sun-hee:	This is my first time. Is it in June every year?
Roberto:	Yeah. Why?
Sun-hee:	Some holidays change. . . like Lunar New Year.
Claudia:	When's that?
Sun-hee:	Sometimes it's in January, but I think this year it's on February second.
Roberto:	Hmm . . . New Year's in February . . . interesting.
Sun-hee:	So what do they do at the Puerto Rican Day Parade?
Claudia:	People sing . . . they dance . . . they wear special costumes. They play lots of cool music . . . and the food is delicious!
Takeshi:	Great! I'm hungry! How long does the parade last?
Roberto:	Well, the parade is from twelve to about three. So it lasts about three hours.
Claudia:	But the celebration lasts until about seven or eight o'clock at night. It's really fun! Come on, the parade starts in fifteen minutes! Let's get moving!
Sun-hee:	Where's the music?
Takeshi:	And the food?
Claudia:	Roberto! Where's the parade?

Roberto:	I know it's today. It's on the second Sunday in June. Let's ask. *(to man on street)* Excuse me? We're looking for the Puerto Rican Day Parade.
Man:	Puerto Rican Day Parade? That's next Sunday. It's on the second Sunday in June.
Roberto:	Yeah but today is . . .
Claudia:	. . . June sixth. The first Sunday in June!
Sun-hee:	So, no dancing?
Claudia:	No cool music?
Takeshi:	And no delicious food? I'm really hungry now. *(noticing nearby Puerto Rican restaurant)* Let's eat!

Unit 8: Global Viewpoints

Special Occasions

Brad:	One of my favorite holidays is the Fourth of July. It is the celebration of the independence of America. I like to go to the park and watch the fireworks.
José Luis:	My favorite holiday is Mexican Independence Day.
Julianna:	My favorite holiday is *Carnaval*. It takes place in February during the summertime. During *Carnaval* I eat *feijoada*, which is a Brazilian traditional dish.
Alejandra:	My favorite holiday is New Year's Eve. After midnight I usually go out with my friends to parties to dance.
Catherine:	My birthday is December seventeenth. Every year my friend throws me a surprise party, and I hate them.
Jackie:	One important Korean holiday we celebrate is *Chusok*. We celebrate *Chusok* by visiting our family members and we also eat *sonphyung*, which is a kind of Korean rice cake, and we also visit our ancestors' graves and ask for blessings.

Unit 9: City Living

Dear Mum and Dad . . .

| Tara: | Dear Mum and Dad. Life in New York is great. My apartment is beautiful and the city is so cool! I'm studying every day and art school is really interesting. My favorite class is art history. I'm working at a café, too. It's not bad, but I'm really busy. I usually work nights but I get up early every day, about seven o'clock. Well . . . maybe 7:30. I get dressed and then I always have a healthy breakfast. Well . . . usually. After |

breakfast I always check my e-mail and I often surf the Net, but only for about an hour. Well. . . sometimes longer. After that I often meet my roommates Sun-hee and Claudia for lunch. Sun-hee is from Korea. She's really nice, and smart! She teaches computer science at New York University. And then there's Claudia. She's so much fun. She's from Rio de Janeiro in Brazil. She's a businesswoman here in New York, so she's really busy. She works from nine to six or seven every day. Anyway, after lunch I always study. Well. . . sometimes I relax a little. I work nights during the week from five to eleven so I go to work at 4:30. I'm never late. OK. Well. . . hardly ever. Then, I get home at about 11:30. Sometimes I do some homework . . . but, not often. I usually just go to bed. Well, not always to bed, but . . . ah . . . don't ask! Give my love to everyone. All the best, Tara.

Unit 9: Global Viewpoints

Daily Activities

Julianna: I get up every day at seven a.m. I take a shower, I brush my teeth. I have breakfast and then I drive to work.

Woo Sung: My sister is a student at New York University. She is studying psychology. She wakes up in the morning, has breakfast and then goes to class.

Hana: My sister is a student. She gets up at nine o'clock in the morning, washes up and then goes to school. After school she has practice for her volleyball team and then she comes home, she studies, she eats, and then she goes to sleep.

Jonathan: I always practice drums for two hours. And then actually at the end of the day I either . . . I usually watch some TV or play some video games and then I go to sleep.

Alejandra: After work, I sometimes go home, and sometimes I meet with friends. Also, sometimes, I go out on dates.

Dating

Alejandra: When I go out on dates, I usually go to the movies or to have dinner or to the theater. On a date we both usually pay.

Hana: I'm 20 years old and I'm single. I have never had a boyfriend.

José Luis: In Mexico, the man usually calls the woman for a date. A woman almost never calls a man. On a date, we usually go to movies and dinner.

Nick: On the weekends, I like to go on dates We usually go to dinner or go to see a movie.

Unit 10: City Living

Welcome to New York!

Sun-hee: So, how did you two become roommates?

Takeshi: Us?

Mike: Well, Tara and I were old friends. So when I moved to New York . . .

Mike: Tara!

Tara: Mike! Welcome to New York! You'll love it here! It's great!

Mike: Maybe, just remember Tara—no apartment, no job—goodbye New York. Got it?

Tara: Don't worry. My friend Takeshi needs a roommate. I'm calling him right now. (into phone) Hi, Takeshi. My friend Mike is in town. He's interested in the apartment. Yes . . . yes . . . OK. (to Mike) It's on the third floor. There are four rooms. There are two bedrooms. There's a big kitchen, and a great living room.

Mike: Is there a bed in the extra bedroom?

Tara: (into phone) Is there a bed for Mike? (to Mike) Yes. The bedroom is furnished. There is a bed, a table, a lamp, a desk . . . and uh . . . there are two chairs.

Mike: Sounds terrific. Let's go!

Tara: (into phone) See you soon!

Takeshi: Hi!

Tara: Hi, Takeshi. This is my friend, Mike.

Takeshi: Hi, Mike.

Mike: Hi.

Takeshi: Come in you two.

Mike: Wow. This is a nice apartment.

Takeshi: Thanks. This is the living room. There's a sofa, a lamp, table . . . TV.

Mike: Nice.

Takeshi: Over there's the kitchen. We have a table. There are a couple of chairs . . . a microwave . . . a fridge.

Takeshi: And here's the bedroom. There's a bed . . . a table, a lamp, a desk . . . and there are two chairs for you.

Mike: I'll take it! Uh . . . how much is the rent?

Takeshi: It's cheap. It's only eight hundred dollars.

Mike: Eight hundred dollars? That's kind of expensive for me. I don't have a job yet!

Tara: Believe me, for New York, that's cheap.

Mike: OK. I'll take it, but just for one or two months.

Takeshi: OK. Welcome home!

Sun-hee:	So that's the story.
Takeshi:	Yep. And two years later, we're still roommates. *(to Mike)* One or two months, huh? *(they laugh)*

Unit 10: Global Viewpoints

Where I Live

Alejandra:	I live in a one-bedroom apartment. It is a small apartment in an old building. In my apartment there is one bedroom, a kitchen, one bathroom, and a living room.
Jackie:	I live in a small house. There are four bedrooms, and a living room. . . kitchen, a dining room.
José Luis:	I live in a house with my parents in Mexico City.
Jonathan:	I live with six other people and there are six rooms, everyone has their own room.
Catherine:	Right now I live with two other roommates. We have three different rooms and a kitchen and that's it. My favorite room in the house is my bedroom.

Student Housing

Hana:	I live in a dorm in my school.
Dave:	I live in a dorm with a roommate. There's not much in it besides myself, my roommate, and two beds. That's all there's room for.
Vanessa:	In my room, I have one roommate and there are two beds, two dressers, and two desks.
Calum:	My dorm is very big and very old. There are a lot of people in my dorm so it's very noisy, especially at night. My dorm room is very small and in the dorm room there is a desk, shelves, an alarm clock, a few books, and a rug.

Unit 11: City Living

What do I wear to the party?

Sun-hee:	Nice suit.
Claudia:	Thanks. Hey, don't forget about Roberto's party tonight.
Sun-hee:	Oh yeah. What kind of party is it?
Claudia:	It's a party for work. All the people from his office are coming. *(running out the door)* See you there!
Sun-hee:	*(to Claudia)* But what do I wear? *(to herself)* Gee, a work party. Roberto's an important businessman . . . sounds pretty formal. . .
Sun-hee:	*(to herself)* Wow. Look at that dress, and these shoes. *(to sales clerk)* Hi.

Sales Clerk:	May I help you?
Sun-hee:	That's a beautiful dress outside.
Sales Clerk:	Oh, which one?
Sun-hee:	The dark one. How much is it?
Sales Clerk:	It's on sale. It's usually two hundred and eighty-five dollars.
Sun-hee:	Two hundred eighty-five dollars? That's pretty expensive.
Sales Clerk:	Yes, but it is on sale. It's only two hundred and twenty-five dollars, and it is a beautiful dress.
Sun-hee:	Two hundred twenty-five. . . that's not a bad price, and it is nice. And those black shoes? How much are they?
Sales Clerk:	They're usually one hundred and twenty-five dollars.
Sun-hee:	A hundred and twenty-five dollars? For shoes?
Sales Clerk:	But, they're on sale for seventy-five.
Sun-hee:	Wow! Seventy-five? That's fifty dollars off! I'll take them.
Sales Clerk:	Great!
Sun-hee:	. . .and the dress too.
Sales Clerk:	Excellent!
Roberto:	Hi!
Mike:	Hi Sun-hee! You look great!
Sun-hee:	Thanks. So, this isn't a formal party?
Roberto:	Hey, don't worry about it. They're just friends from work. Besides, Mike dressed up!
Mike:	*(flashing tuxedo design T-shirt)* Look!
Roberto:	Come on in.

Unit 11: Global Viewpoints

Fashion and Colors

Paula:	I like fashion. I like to dress up well, but fashion is not everything.
Brad:	This is my favorite shirt. I love it because it is yellow and bright. This shirt only cost five dollars. I bought it at a used clothing store.
Dave:	My favorite article of clothing is, of course, my shoes. They're about five years old. I bought them for about twenty dollars.
Catherine:	I like to wear casual clothes like jeans and a sweatshirt, but at work I have to wear more formal clothing, like trousers or suits. I like to wear bright colors but I also like to wear black too.
Dennis:	I'm a very informal dresser, so I feel more relaxed wearing jeans. I love to wear black, because it makes me look thin.
Hana:	I like to wear black, purple, and white.

Julianna: My favorite colors are black and red, just like this.

Alejandra: My favorite piece of clothing is my scarf that my grandmother made for me, and it's really warm.

Shopping

Catherine: I like to shop a lot.

Brad: I shop on the Internet. Usually I buy computers, software, and video games.

Alejandra: I don't shop on the Internet, because I don't know about the sizes.

Hana: I don't shop on the Internet because my mom told me not to.

Unit 12: City Living

I can get this job!

Mike: I can't do this.

Roberto: Yes, you can!

Mike: No, I can't!

Roberto: It's just a job interview.

Mike: Yes, but I really want this job!

Roberto: What time is the interview?

Mike: It's today at three o'clock.

Roberto: Don't worry. I have some time before my appointment. I can help you.

Mike: What are you doing?

Roberto: I'm interviewing you. I'm a businessman. Trust me. I know this. Sit down. *(imitating interviewer)* Welcome, Mr. Johnson. Do you have your resume?

Mike: Yes. Here you are Mr. Chavez. *(aside to Roberto)* How am I doing?

Roberto: You're doing fine. Just relax. *(imitating interviewer)* Very interesting. Let's see. An actor, a waiter, a painter, a singer, a receptionist. Wow, that's a lot of jobs. So, are you looking for a full-time or a part-time job?

Mike: Full-time . . . or part-time. I'm flexible.

Roberto: I see. What do you do now?

Mike: Well, I don't have a job right now.

Roberto: *(as himself)* No, no, no. Don't say that. Say "I'm between jobs." Now. . .

Mike: *(to himself)* I'm between jobs . . .OK. Yeah.

Roberto: *(imitating interviewer)* Tell me about yourself. What are you like?

Mike: Well, I'm smart, and creative . . .

Roberto: *(as himself)* That's good! That's good! Sell yourself! Tell them about your good points!

Mike: OK. And I'm funny and outgoing. . . definitely not shy.

Roberto: That's great. *(imitating interviewer)* OK. What languages do you speak?

Mike: I speak Spanish, but I can't write it very well.

Roberto: OK. What else can you do?

Mike: I can use PCs and Macs.

Roberto: *(as himself)* That's great, get excited!

Mike: And I'm very hardworking . . . and I know I can get this job!

Roberto: That's right! Now go get 'em! Hey, by the way, what kind of job interview is this?

Mike: It's a job for a lifeguard down at the city pool.

Roberto: A lifeguard? Can you swim?

Mike: No, I can't. But I look good in a bathing suit!

Unit 12: Global Viewpoints

My Job

Brad: I'm a student, but I also have a part-time job. I'm a computer technician and I help students and teachers fix their computers

Vanessa: I have two jobs. I have a job at a bank, and a job at the mall in a store. I'm a teller at the bank. At my second job, at the store where I work, I am a cashier.

Kumiko: I teach Japanese language to non-Japanese students. I like my job because it's so much fun.

Julianna: I am a financial manager. I like my job because I like to work with numbers.

Catherine: I like being a lawyer because I get to help people. I also like being a lawyer because you get to talk a lot and I like to talk. To be a lawyer you have to be very organized, hardworking, and also quick-thinking.

Alejandra: I work as an international student advisor. I help international students at universities. I love my job because I meet a lot of interesting people.

People at Work

Brad: I work in an office with three others. They are hardworking and friendly.

Vanessa: The people that I work with are very funny and outgoing.

Kumiko: My co-teachers are friendly, hardworking, and sometimes very serious.

Alejandra: The people I work with are very hardworking but not serious.